mana g
with intent

managing

with intent

Ian Mann

ZEBRA

Published by Zebra Press
an imprint of Random House Struik (Pty) Ltd
Company Reg. No. 1966/003153/07
80 McKenzie Street, Cape Town, 8001
PO Box 1144, Cape Town, 8000, South Africa

www.zebrapress.co.za

First published 2002
Reprinted in 2004, 2005 (twice), 2006 and 2008

7 9 10 8 6

Publication © Zebra Press 2002
Text © Ian Mann 2002

Publisher: Marlene Fryer
Managing editor: Robert Plummer
Cover and text designer: Natascha Adendorff-Olivier
Typesetter: Natascha Adendorff-Olivier

Set in 11 pt on 14 pt ITC Veljovic

Reproduction by Hirt & Carter (Cape) (Pty) Ltd
Printed and bound by Paarl Print, Oosterland Street, Paarl, South Africa

ISBN 978 1 86872 655 4

Contents

Introduction

If you read this book like any other book, you will not be any better at managing than you are now. You might find out a few things, but don't worry, you'll soon forget them. You will still have trouble with staff, you will still want to do and say things that never get done or said. If you read this book like any other book, you'll be no better because of it – I promise you.

If, however, you want this book to improve your ability to manage other people effectively, and to get the right things done in the most constructive way, then you must work with it! This book cannot do it for you – you have to do it for yourself. Don't sit back and relax! Take ownership of the material, understand it, make it your own, get involved with the ideas, and, most importantly, try them out. Practise them, note what goes right and what goes wrong, and learn from this.

If you do this, you will become a more professional manager, and you will enjoy your work more, feel more satisfied and get more done. In the beginning, as you try out the material, it may feel unnatural, but when you are comfortable with it, you will feel the power of managing with intent.

MEMORY AND UNDERSTANDING

Look at the numbers below. Concentrate on them for a minute, then close the book and see if you can remember them.

1 4 9 1 6 2 5 3 6 4 9 6 4 8 1

Could you remember the numbers? And would you be able to remember them in a week's time? Probably not. It looks like a random list of numbers that is almost impossible to remember. People remember most easily when they understand.

Studies have shown that if a Grand Master looks at a chessboard, with pieces placed just anywhere, they have a hard time remembering the position of the pieces on the board. But if you show them a game in play, they have no difficulty remembering the board. People remember most easily what they understand.

I am going to show you how to memorise those numbers so that if you were asked to repeat them in a week's time – or in five years' time – you would be able to do so with ease.

The numbers are the squares of a sequence of numbers from 1 to 9: $1 \times 1 = 1$, $2 \times 2 = 4$, $3 \times 3 = 9$, $4 \times 4 = 16$, $5 \times 5 = 25$, and so on. Now if I asked you these numbers in five years' time, you would be able to remember them easily, wouldn't you?

INTRODUCTION TO THE ARCH

Let me explain why I showed you those numbers. The connection between memory and understanding applies to being a better manager. Management is a real-time activity: there is no opportunity to reflect or check your notebook. You have to function from very deeply held ideas that are part of who you are. The management model I'm going to show you is easy to remember and easy to use, and when you use it repeatedly it will become part of how you look at the world.

The model is an arch, made of five blocks. Each part of the arch is an aspect that can help or hinder your effectiveness as a manager. Let's look at these components one by one.

1. Clarity

The arch rests on two foundation pillars. Let's look at the one on the left first: 'clarity'.

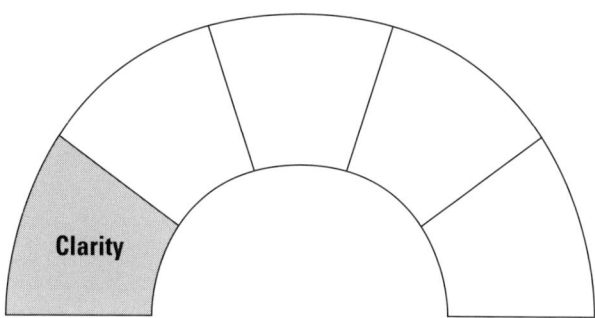

When a staff member is not performing well, the first thing you have to check for is clarity: Am I clear about what I want from this person? And are they clear about what I want? First you have to be clear about what you want, and then you have to make that clear to the staff member.

Extensive research shows that most managers aren't clear about what they want from their staff. A consultant who was commissioned to implement a performance appraisal system in a company told me that she would ask the manager to identify what he wanted from the employee. Then she would ask the employee to write down what the manager wanted from him. Countless times she would go back to the manager just to check that she was talking to the right person, because the two lists had nothing in common! The manager had quite obviously never communicated his requirement in a way that the staff member could understand, or their lists would have been the same.

Without clarity, it is very difficult to get anything done. But there are ways of solving the problem. In this book I will show you how to deal with issues like this in the real world of work.

2. Commitment

Sometimes the staff member knows exactly what to do – there is no problem with that. They just don't care. If that is the case, you have a commitment problem. This is the second component of the arch.

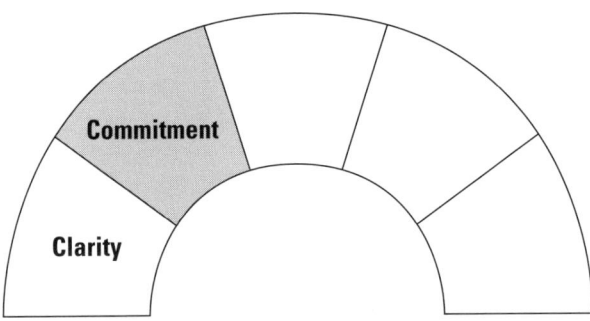

So often we see people who joined a company straight after school, and were given a relatively undemanding set of tasks, and ten years later they are still doing the same work. Because of their level they are never involved in any decisions, they are never challenged and they feel quite alienated from their employers. There is nothing about their work that motivates them; by now it is just a mindless routine. A job is a job and they don't think about it much at work and certainly not when they leave work. They are usually given no attention unless something has gone wrong.

If you know that the problem is a clarity problem you can solve it. If you know it is a commitment problem you can fix that too. The challenge is to get the staff member to want to do what you want them to do, and I will show you how to do that.

3. Self-Image

At the centre of the arch is self-image. It is possible that the staff member knows exactly what to do, and they are committed, but still they don't perform. The reason could be a self-image problem. People don't perform above or below their self-image.

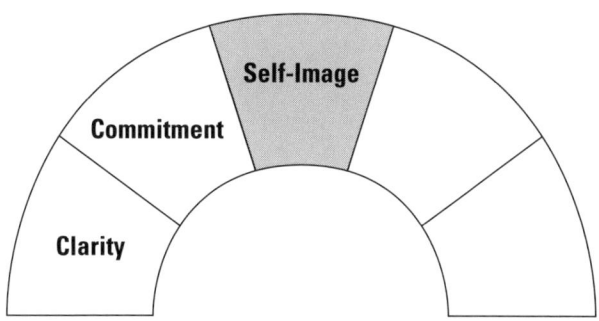

If you ask someone to do something above their self-image, they won't do it. If you ask a young, introverted employee to give a talk in front of the entire company, with the managing director present, what do you think he is going to do? He will probably fall sick all of a sudden, or find some other excuse. His self-image does not allow him to stand up in front of so many people and give a talk.

In the same way, if you ask someone to do something that is below their self-image, they won't do it either. Picture a secretary: she is well dressed and well groomed. You say to her, 'My car is absolutely filthy and I am taking the MD out this afternoon; can you sort it out?' She says, 'Sure, where are the keys and where is the nearest car wash?'

'No,' you say. 'I don't mean take it to a car wash. There is a bucket and a hose in the garage, and I have a cloth in the boot. Wash it there.' What do you think she is going to say to you?

People don't do things that are beneath them if they can possibly help it. Now, if she was only a temp who might be considered for a permanent position, and if she was struggling to find her ex-husband and his maintenance cheque, things might be different. She might go down to the garage and wash your car. But it would not break her heart if there was some grit on the cloth that could scratch the paint of your car!

People don't want to do things that are above or below their self-image, and if they do, they usually do so reluctantly and without enthusiasm.

4. Price

Let's consider another problem. At a liquor store, the computer system goes down for a few days just before month-end. When it goes back on line, the admin manager asks his staff to work a few hours overtime each night for the rest of the week so they can get back on track for month-end. They all refuse. The manager is outraged. These women always complain that they don't have enough money, he fumes, and now that they are given a chance to make overtime money, they are too lazy to take it!

Let's apply the arch to this problem and see how it works. The women know exactly why they are being asked to stay late, so it isn't a clarity problem. It doesn't seem to be a commitment problem either. They often work through their lunch break in busy times, and they seem to like the company. And since they are being asked to do what they normally do, it can't be a self-image problem. What else could it be?

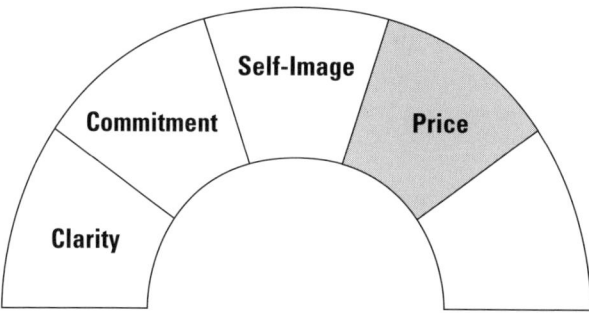

The next part of the arch is price. The price in this context is not money; it is what it costs the person to do what is being asked. What is the price these women would have to pay to stay late each night? Most of them live in a rough neighbourhood quite far away from the store. To travel there by train at 9:30 at night is called 'kill me quick!' There is no way these women would stay late; they are not stupid: going home that late is just too dangerous. In their case it is a price problem. They won't stay late because the price is too high.

Of course, once you know what the price is, it is often easy to work out a solution. All the manager has to do is arrange a taxi to take the women to their homes and instruct the driver to wait until they are safely indoors. Then there will be no problem with them working late, and they'll happily do so.

5. Behaviour

If a staff member is not performing and it is not a clarity problem, or a commitment, self-image or price problem, then it is simply a behaviour problem. Behaviour is what a person does, not what they think or feel. If a person's behaviour is inappropriate, they will not get the right things done.

All too often managers jump to the conclusion that the problem is a behaviour problem without examining the other four possibilities first. It is a behaviour problem if the person does not know how to do the job as required. This could be the result of a lack of skills or knowledge. Or the person could have developed bad habits, so their behaviour is inappropriate. Behaviour can be corrected by means of feedback and training.

In the high-pressured world of business today, people are often placed in jobs hastily, with only the briefest explanation of what they have to do, and then they are required to perform. They are not guided, there is little support, and they are expected to sink or swim. They are left to guess what they are required to do, and hopefully learn by trial and error. Their manager, who understands the job well, has underestimated the complexity of the task and how long it would take a new person to work it out for themselves.

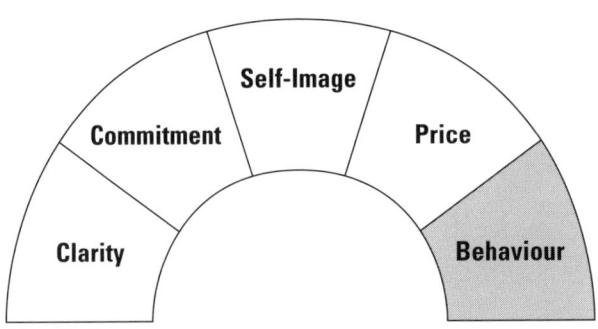

When you manage your staff you will have problems getting the right things done – it's normal, it's natural, it is to be expected, and it is very annoying! Too many managers simply give up and say, 'My staff are useless! How am I supposed to manage with this bunch of turkeys?' But, by using the arch, the professional manager can identify what the problem is and find appropriate solutions.

The arch will guide you to identify areas in which your staff are not performing well and show you how to correct those areas. In the chapters that follow, I will explain how.

1

Clarity

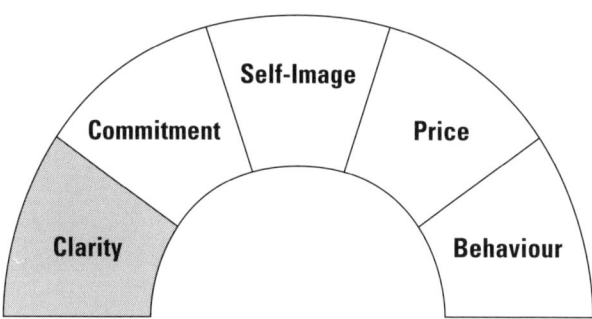

In this chapter we will look at the first part of the arch – the left-hand side, the issue of clarity. If you have a problem with a staff member's performance, the first questions to ask are about clarity: Am I clear about what I want from this person? And is the person clear about what they are supposed to do?

There are two sides to clarity. First, you have to be clear about what you want as a manager, and, second, you have to make your staff clear about what you want. You cannot make your staff clear unless you are clear yourself. Let's start by clarifying exactly what managers do.

WHAT MANAGERS DO

In order to be a highly effective manager, you have to understand how management has changed over time. If somebody was an excellent manager 25 years ago, he or she might well be an awful manager today, because the guiding principles of good management have changed. Let me explain why this is so.

Authority, Power and Influence

There are three energies with which we can control the behaviour of other people. These are authority, power and influence.[1]

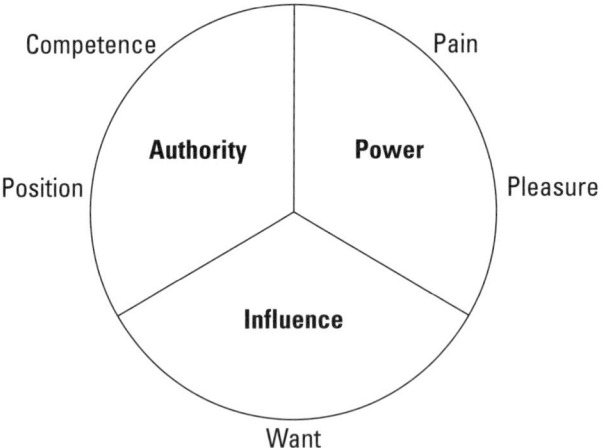

When most people think about controlling the behaviour of others, whether it is at the workplace, at home, with friends or in the community, they think in terms of having power.

Let's look at what power is. Power has two parts to it: pain and pleasure. You have power over other people to the extent that you can cause them pain or give them pleasure. If you cannot hurt or help a person, you have absolutely no power over them.

We can cause pain or pleasure in a range of ways, from subtle to severe. You can inflict pain on people in the workplace simply by ignoring them or being unfriendly, making them feel insulted or embarrassed. More seriously, you could overlook someone for promotion, give them unpleasant work, or make their working conditions difficult. You can give someone pleasure simply by being friendly, or by giving them growth and learning opportunities, or interesting work that they enjoy thoroughly. If you are able to inflict pain on somebody or give them pleasure, in the workplace or anywhere else, then you have power over them.

The second way of controlling people's behaviour is authority. There are two kinds of authority, the first of which is authority from position. This comes from your position in the company – or in the home, or wherever – which entitles you to do things that you wouldn't be able to do if you didn't have that position. If you are a manager there are certain things that you are entitled to do, which you couldn't do if you weren't a manager. If you are the father or mother in the house, there are things that you can do that you couldn't do if you were the child. This authority comes from position, if you have that position.

The second source of authority is competence. People have authority over others simply because they are competent. Imagine that you are sitting at home one night, working on your computer, putting the finishing touches on a long report for work, and the screen goes blank. 'It's gone!' you shout. 'All my work is gone!' And your fourteen-year-old daughter says, 'No, it doesn't just *go*. Get back to the C drive and check up on Windows Explorer. Search for the name of the document ...' Whatever the child tells you to do, you do exactly. In fact, if she told you to lean forward and kiss the screen three times, you would probably do that as well. The child is able to control your behaviour, because she has authority over you – authority that comes from competence. Exactly the same thing happens when the managing director listens to the computer technician, who is in a lower position than him but knows more than him when it comes to computers. And of course, the same applies when a staff member does what the manager suggests because of her respect for the manager's competence. We listen to people because we believe in their competence.

The last energy we use to control the behaviour of others is influence. The word associated with this energy is 'want'. You have influenced another person if – and only if – they want to do what you want them to do. If they do what you say because they are afraid of you, you have used power. If they do it because you are the manager, you have used authority from position. But if they do it because they personally want to do it, then you have influenced them.

Influence is getting another human being to want to do what you want them to do. Even if your back is turned, even if you are out of the office for the whole day, they will continue to do it, because they want to.

Management Today vs. 1911

The job of a manager is to get staff to do what has to be done. The manager can do this by means of power, authority and influence. But the proportions of these three energies have changed over the years.

Let's go back nearly 100 years, to 1911. The reason I'm choosing 1911 is that this was when the first serious book on management was written. Human beings have been managing for centuries. In the first century, in the year one, when Dad was working the fields with his three sons, telling them what to do and how to do it, he was managing people. But it wasn't until 1911 that we ever wrote down how we think people should manage.

The very first book dedicated exclusively to management, the first guide on how to manage better, came out in 1911. The book was called *The Principles of Scientific Management* and was written by a man called Frederick Taylor. Essentially, what he said was that the core of management is organising, planning and controlling.

For many, many years – in fact, for most of the twentieth century

– we have been thinking of organising, planning and controlling as the core of good management. But that view is very old-fashioned. Today, if all you did was organise, plan and control, you would probably be a very poor manager.

In 1911, a manager could walk onto the factory floor, point to an employee, and say: 'You – not you, the other man, *you* – I don't like your attitude! Get your jacket, take your pay packet, and get the hell out of here and don't come back!' The man would be shocked, but he'd pick up his jacket, collect his pay from the pay counter, and walk out of the factory forever.

In 1911, how big would power, authority and influence be, as slices of the managerial pie?

Managerial energies 1911

The largest slices of the pie were power and authority. Influence was a very, very small part of the pie. In 1911 the managers didn't need to, nor did they, care whether their workers wanted to do the job. They managed primarily through power and authority – and this authority was authority from position.

Let's contrast that to managing today. How does management work today in terms of the managerial pie?

Managerial energies today

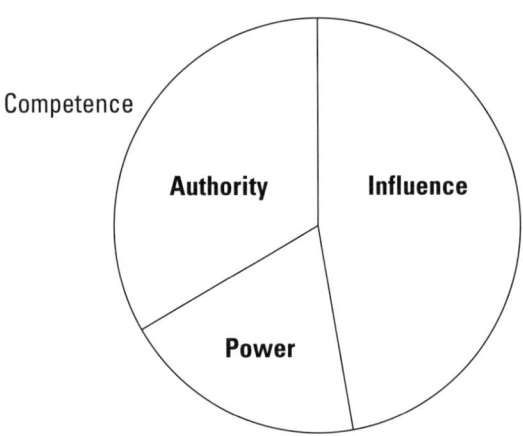

The pie looks very different. You'll agree that the smallest slice today is power. We have very little power over other people in the workplace today. This is the result of many factors. One is the strength and maturity of unionism, another is labour legislation, and a third is that society as a whole has moved away from the idea of power.

Authority is a large slice of the pie, but this is authority that comes primarily, although not exclusively, from competence. You can't say, 'Take your jacket, take your pay and get out of here' – if for no other reason other than that legislation won't allow it. People nowadays will listen to people because of their competence far faster than they will listen to people because of their position.

A large part of the pie today is influence, your ability to get other people to want to do what you want them to do. It is vital to use influence in your managerial style. In 1911 we didn't need to learn how to influence other people. Today we do. Influence is probably the most essential ingredient in effective management.

You need clarity on the context of management today. If you had a 1911 style of management, how you would perform would be very different from how you'd perform if you practised today's management style. What might have been appropriate in the past is no longer acceptable today. We cannot manage using power and authority from position; we have to move strongly over to influence and authority from competence.

Managing Volunteers

If you've ever been involved in some sort of voluntary work – for your community, for your church, for your sports club, for your child's school – you will know the difference between managing a group of volunteers and a group of employees. Volunteers believe in what they do, they enjoy what they do, and we have no control over them. Volunteers will work only if they want to. Volunteers have to want to do the work.

Here is a guiding principle in your management of people. Imagine that all who work for you are volunteers. Imagine how you would manage if you treated all your employees as volunteers.

This is a fresh way of looking at staff. It highlights the need for winning them over and getting them committed. Volunteers want to be part of the action. That is why they are there, and they can withdraw their efforts if they choose to. Staff can also withdraw, and when they do, they often stay on the payroll!

Task and People

When you manage other people, there are two things that you have to pay attention to – task and people. If you take your eye off either of these two things, you will not be a successful manager.

'Task' means getting the job done – nothing more, nothing less. Managers are charged with seeing to it that the tasks they manage get done. You must have clarity about what the task is and how to do it.

You also need to pay attention to people. Note that I say 'people', not 'person'. There is a good reason for this. Nowadays people everywhere are interdependent: one person depends on another person in order to fulfil their tasks. If I can't do my job well unless you do your job well, then I am dependent on you, and if you can't do your work well unless I do my work well, then you are dependent on me, and the two of us together are interdependent.

You don't just manage people in isolation; the people you manage have to work with others. They need to be able to get on with each other and rely on each other. The last thing a manager wants is staff who spend most of their day fighting with one another instead of getting the job done.

Look at the graph on the next page. The first manager focuses only on the task and not on people. This person is called 'the dictator', and he or she will have underperforming staff. A good manager has to worry about how his or her people feel, how they get on with each other, their welfare, their growth, their happiness, and so on. Management is all about people, because it is the people who get the task done for you. If you don't have positive people you will never succeed on the task side.

But the manager who focuses only on people – the manager we call 'the social worker' – will also have problems. Very simply, he or she will have happy staff, but nothing will get done. The good manager – 'the star' – focuses on both. And a manager who focuses on neither is 'dazed and confused' – this person shouldn't be a manager at all.

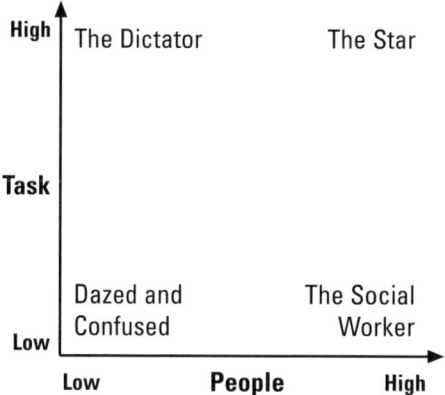

As a manager, you need to understand this notion of 'task' and 'people' because you have to focus on both all the time. If you fail at one of these aspects, you have failed overall, even if you are superb at the other.

If this sounds obvious, remember that the guiding principles of traditional management were organising, planning and controlling – nothing about keeping your people happy and motivated.

You have to be clear about what management today is all about. If a person believed that good management was only organising, planning and controlling, then the goals they would set for themselves would be limited to those areas. Their goals would be very different if they believed management is about influencing rather than power and control, and that it involves an equal focus on the people aspects and the task aspects. Those managers who still cling to old, outdated concepts will find it more and more difficult to manage well and to get ahead in a people-centred work environment.

GETTING STAFF CLEAR

As a manager, you have to be absolutely clear about what you want. If you are not, you must understand that you will never ever get anybody else clear. You cannot make something clear to other people unless it is first clear to you. That is perfectly obvious – but it's not something that is commonly done.

The other side of the coin is making your ideas perfectly clear to other people. The clearer it is to them, the easier it will be for them to do what you want them to do.

Responsibility for Communication

Here is the golden rule of communication and the platinum rule of management:

Communication is 100 per cent the responsibility of the person speaking.

Not 50 per cent the responsibility of the person speaking and 50 per cent the responsibility of the person listening. It is 100 per cent the responsibility of the speaker. It is his or her responsibility to cause the other person to understand what he or she is saying. If the person isn't listening, it is the speaker's responsibility to attract their attention and to get them to listen. If the listener doesn't have the necessary vocabulary or knowledge, the onus is on the speaker to talk in such a way that the person understands.

When you started your first job, you may have had an experience like this. Your manager or supervisor walks over to you and mutters something about something he wants you to do. 'Sure,' you say, and as soon as he walks away, you turn to one of your colleagues and ask, 'What was he talking about?' You believed that the responsibility for the communication was on you, the listener, not on the speaker. You believed it was your responsibility to read your manager's mind so that you would know exactly what he was talking about. You didn't say: 'I don't understand what you are trying to tell me.' You thought that you didn't understand because you were stupid, and the last thing you wanted to do was let him find out that you were stupid, so soon. The reality is that the onus of communication is 100 per cent on the speaker. It is the speaker's task to make sure that the listener understands. This is particularly important because communication is such a complex process.

The Complexity of Communication

It is difficult to get people to do what you tell them, because communication is so complex. It is vital that you understand this fact. Let's take a very simple example, a single word: 'chair'. If I ask you to picture a chair in your mind, what do you see? You might see an office chair, or a rocking chair, or the La-Z-Boy you sit on when you watch TV. Another reader would picture something different.

If I say the word 'chair', different people will get different images in their minds. But a chair is a very simple thing. Imagine the differences in people's minds when we talk about complicated things like budgets, projects or client service. Now imagine a new staff member's understanding of these concepts. Their perception of the task is likely to be very different from what you intended. If most people are poor communicators, this is because they have never given any thought to how complicated communication really is. The sooner we understand the difficulty involved in communication, the better communicators we will be.

Media of Communication

If people were computers, it would be very easy to communicate. If you download information from one computer's C drive onto a stiffy disk, insert the disk into another computer and copy it onto the C drive, the second computer will receive exactly the same information easily, simply and without any error. (Most of the time, anyway!) But with people it doesn't work that easily. With people we have to use a medium, something to connect them to one another in order to get information across.

There are several ways in which we get information across. Some are appropriate for certain types of instructions, others are not. If you want to give somebody a 25-point shopping list, for example, speech is a very poor way to communicate, because they are going to forget and get muddled. Giving a written list is a far better way of doing it. If, on the other hand, you want to discuss complicated ideas – like the overall goals of a project or a new service campaign – the easiest way to do it is through speaking face to face.

We can also communicate by using gestures. Perhaps you are saying goodbye to a very dear friend who is going away to work in another city, and you shake their hand in the airport departure lounge. Shaking hands is a gesture. You shake their hand and hold it a little longer, a little tighter, and in that gesture you are saying more than you could possibly say in speech. You are saying: 'I am going to miss you. You are important to me. This is difficult for me.' And you are saying it much more efficiently than you could with words. Sometimes gestures are absolutely necessary. If you need to communicate with someone on the opposite side of a rugby field, the only way is by waving or giving signs.

When you want to communicate complex things like the company's financial performance over the past twelve months, a graph would be the best way to describe it. If you're representing the reporting structure of a company, you could use a diagram.

There are different media of communication – verbal, non-verbal, writing and illustrations – and each of these is more efficient for different kinds of communication.

But it gets even more complicated than this, because people differ in the way they take in information. If you read out a 25-point shopping list, most people would not remember all the items. But some people can. Their usual way of taking in information is by listening, and they obviously have very good memories. But remembering long lists is not easy for most people. That's not surprising: it is an unusual ability.

Other people tend not to take in information by listening. Some of them understand instructions better if they are written down, and others understand best when they see graphs or diagrams.

The important point is that giving tasks to people is a very complex process. Different tasks need to be communicated by different media, and each person's method of understanding must be considered. You need to be aware of the differences in the way people take in information so you can use this to enhance communication.

Barriers to Communication

On top of this, there are any number of barriers that prevent people from understanding each other. Even if you are communicating clearly, it is perfectly possible that the other person won't get your meaning accurately or at all.

Barriers to communication can come from absolutely anywhere. The person might not be paying attention, they might not know the vocabulary or jargon that you are using, or they might not understand the work. They might not understand your accent because you are not speaking in their home language – or yours.

In order to communicate clearly to people, you have to understand the barriers that stand in the way of clear communication. Communication is not simple, but to be an effective manager you have to be an effective communicator. There is no way that your staff will be able to mind-read what you expect from them. You have to communicate what you want clearly and distinctly.

Your Staff's Level of Development

Even if you recognise the complexity of communication, do your best to overcome the barriers to communication, and give an instruction clearly and distinctly, the person might still not get the message. Why not? It all has to do with their stage of development in their particular job.

When someone is hired by a company or promoted to a new position, they lack experience and will need a lot of guidance. As the months and years go by, they become more experienced and more competent. Eventually, after a few years, they become supremely competent and know their job inside-out.

It stands to reason that you can't talk the same way to people who are at different stages of development. A manager who does so is a poor manager. You can talk to people the same way, but you must understand that they will simply not understand you in the same way. You cannot possibly communicate with somebody who is just starting in a job the same way you would communicate with somebody who has been there a long time.

The inexperienced person needs lots and lots of direction; you will have to be very clear and precise in your instructions. If, on the other hand, the person is highly experienced, you can even mutter or mumble an instruction. They will respond, 'Yes' – and 'Yes' from a highly experienced person means: 'The job will be done perfectly as it has been done every year for the last thirteen years, and if there are any problems I will let you know that I have solved them.'

It is important to remember that the level of development says nothing about the human being. It says something about the human being *in a particular situation* and *for a particular task*. A staff member who has been doing a job for two or three years, who is highly competent, might be promoted to a higher position or moved into a different part of the business. Now they have different work to do, and all of a sudden they are inexperienced again and need a lot of guidance.

CRIS

Now I'd like to introduce you to an important model, a checklist for communicating effectively. I call this model 'CRIS' – it is an acronym for the four aspects of effective communication.

> **(C)** heck for clarity of communication
>
> **(R)** eporting structure
>
> **(I)** nvolve
>
> **(S)** et standards

Any time you have a problem communicating with somebody, it's almost always because you didn't do something that forms part of the CRIS checklist.

Check for Clarity of Communication

Let's begin with the 'C' – checking for clarity of communication. When you give someone an instruction, it is your responsibility to check that they have understood what you were talking about.

A researcher told me the following story. He was doing a climate survey for a company in another city, and had just taken on a young assistant researcher to help him. He was due to meet with the company directors at the end of the week, at three o'clock on Friday afternoon, to give them feedback on his findings. On the Monday morning before that, he went to Rudolf, the assistant researcher, and said: 'Here is the data; please would you let me have it in an organised form?' Rudolf said, 'No problem.' (Rudolf always said, 'No problem.') That evening the researcher asked Rudolf, 'How are you doing?' and Rudolf said, 'Getting on nicely.' 'Good,' he said, and he left.

In the course of the week, whenever he bumped into Rudolf, he asked him how the research was going. Rudolf said that it was more work than he had expected, but – as always – 'No problem.' By the time the researcher was about to leave for the airport on Wednesday,

Rudolf still wasn't finished, but he promised to send the research with a colleague who was going to travel to the same city the following day. But by this time he still wasn't finished.

The researcher was shocked. It was Thursday evening, and he was presenting his findings to a valued client the next day. He started thinking about how he was going to do Rudolf grievous bodily harm when he got hold of him! He was going to kill him so many times, he'd wish he was dead already.

But simply being angry with Rudolf wasn't going to help. He had to devise a plan – and this is what he did. He wrote up seven pages of notes on how to do the research in half a day, using two people. In his notes he said everything from 'Switch the computer on, press this button, if the light isn't on, then check the plug.' He left absolutely nothing to chance. He knew that Estelle, a secretary, always came in early, so he faxed the notes to her and asked her to get hold of Rudolf so they could do the work together. The two of them finished in half a day what Rudolf hadn't managed to finish in four days. At half past one they e-mailed the completed information to the researcher. He was able to put his presentation together and meet with the executives at three o'clock.

All weekend he thought about how he was going to yell and scream at Rudolf, until it dawned on him that had he given him the seven pages of notes the Monday before, Rudolf probably would have finished by Tuesday. But he hadn't: he hadn't checked for clarity of communication. So, when he came back to the office, he simply said to Rudolf, 'These things happen.'

The first part of any effective communication is checking for the clarity of the communication. How can you check whether somebody has understood you? The most effective way is simply to ask them if they have understood. You can do this in lots of different ways. You don't have to say: 'I want to check whether you have understood, so tell me what I have just said.' You have to work out a way that feels comfortable and natural. You might say, 'Well, how are you going to handle this now?' And based on what they tell you, you have a good sense of whether they understand. Or you could simply ask them to repeat your instructions. Whatever you feel comfortable with and whatever is appropriate for the person you are talking to.

Reporting Structure

The 'R' in CRIS stands for reporting structure. *What you expect*, they say, *you must inspect*. If you expect people to do something, you must check that they have done it – that's what we mean by a reporting structure. You must know whether the person has done what you asked them to do or not, and you must know if things are going as planned or if there are problems. If you simply give someone a task and expect them to do it, and get angry when you find out two months later that it hasn't been done, you simply haven't used the second part of CRIS, which is establishing a reporting structure.

The reporting structure is based on the person's level of development in their job. If they are relatively new and inexperienced, you have to be very specific in your instruction and you would probably set up a reporting structure like this: 'Before you take tea this morning, come to me and let me know how much you have done.' That way they can only make mistakes on one-and-a-half hours' work. Then you tell them to show you their work before lunch and before afternoon tea. That way you are absolutely sure that very little can go wrong and you will also be helping them enormously in their development.

If, on the other hand, they have been doing the job for years and are highly competent at it, you simply tell them what to do and say, 'Before year-end or before month-end, just let me know you have finished it' – and they will say, 'Yes.' And as we said, 'Yes' from a highly experienced person means: 'It will be done correctly and if there are any problems, I will let you know that I have solved them.'

If somebody has been in the job for several months, you might want to tell them to let you know where they are up to at the end of each day, and someone who's been in the job for a year or two, maybe at the end of each week. We devise our reporting structure based on the development level of the person, so you don't find yourself checking up every hour and a half on somebody who is highly experienced and you don't leave an inexperienced person to sink or swim – which usually means sink!

Involve

The 'I' in CRIS stands for involve. You need to ask the person their opinion. One reason for this is that people who are involved are more committed. Another reason is that the person might have a very good idea about how to do the task, and since they are going to have to do it, they are probably more likely than you to see the obstacles and solutions. If you ask someone to move a pile of goods and you are clear that they know where it should be moved from, when it should be moved, how it should be moved and so on, then you say to them: 'Are you going to be able to do this? Have you got any ideas?' The person might say: 'If I had another person to help me, I would be able to finish this in fifteen minutes. If I do it on my own, it will probably take me two hours.' You say: 'Good thinking; get yourself somebody to give you a hand!'

Set Standards

The last part of the CRIS acronym – the 'S' – is setting standards. Even though standards are part of the task, they are so important that we need to think about them separately, as a special issue. If you ask somebody to tidy up the conference room, what does this mean? Does it mean straighten the desks and tidy it up slightly so it will be ready for us to come back to tomorrow morning? Or vacuum and polish it because there are VIPs coming to visit this evening? Unless you set standards and make your standards absolutely clear to people, don't expect them to know what the standards are.

Whenever you have a communication breakdown, whether it is at work or at home, with employees, suppliers, family or friends, it is probably because you failed at one of the four aspects of CRIS. Perhaps you did not check for clarity of communication. Or you did not establish a reporting structure to find out if things were going wrong. You might not have involved the person sufficiently, so you did not get their buy-in and their perception of the problems and solutions. Or you did not set appropriate standards, and as a result the work was done, but not to the standards you wanted.

Here's an example. You ask a messenger to collect a parcel of documents from the company lawyer. 'Sure,' he says. An hour later you see him still in the office, so you say, 'Didn't I tell you to go to the lawyer?' 'I'm going,' he says. Then you probably get angry and say, 'When I ask you to do something I expect you to do it!' But, in fact, you didn't communicate very well.

If you used CRIS it would have gone something like this: 'I want you to go to the lawyer now and collect a parcel of important documents that I require urgently. The lawyer has left them with his receptionist because he may be out the office. Her name is Cynthia. It is most important that I get the documents before 12:00 because I need them for a meeting this afternoon and I have to review them. I would like you to go right away, and when you come back, I don't want you to leave the parcel with my secretary as you would usually do, I want you to bring it directly to me. Are you going to be able to do that for me?'

If your messenger says, 'But I have two other errands for Dirk and William that they have asked me to do today, and they asked before you,' you might say, 'You go now and take care of the lawyer and I'll take care of explaining to them why this is so urgent.' Then you ask:

'Do you have the lawyer's address? Have you been there before? Should I write down the name of the receptionist for you?' If he says, 'I've been there a few times, and I know Cynthia,' you know he understands. Then you might ask: 'How long do you think you will be?' If he says, 'I can be back in an hour, and I will bring it to you directly,' you know he has understood the urgency and what he has to do.

What have you done? C, you have checked for clarity of communication. R, you have set up a reporting structure: he is going to bring the documents to you immediately. I, you have involved him, when you asked him if he could do the task. S, you have set standards: you told him to bring the documents to you as soon as he gets back and not leave them with your secretary. You want to see to it that whenever you are communicating you communicate clearly.

In order to follow these steps effectively, you must do so in a way that is natural to you. If you say, 'Okay, C – I'm checking for clarity of communication' and 'R – here is your reporting structure,' and so on, people will think you are crazy. You have to communicate using CRIS in a way that is perfectly natural to you.

In fact, the reality is that you are unlikely to remember to do this before you give an instruction. Normal people don't work like that. The real value of this format doesn't lie in remembering to do it before you talk, it lies in the analysis when things go wrong. When things go wrong, and you are reflecting on why they did, you should ask yourself which part of CRIS you didn't use. You will probably find it is the same thing every time – you don't check for clarity, or don't involve the person, or whatever. The real value comes in when you notice that you are always failing at one of the four; then you become aware of it and you start attending to it naturally. That's where the value lies.

We started off by saying the arch is a model that we use for managing people. The first question you always have to ask yourself, when you are having difficulty with a staff member, is: Is clarity the problem? Am I clear about what I want, and have I made myself clear to the other person?

Think about your staff, and ask yourself if they are absolutely clear about what you want from them. It is perfectly possible that you haven't made yourself clear, because up till now you probably weren't particularly clear yourself. This isn't something to be alarmed at. Being clear is just something that you haven't done yet. It isn't automatic. It happens only after you have applied the techniques that you've learnt in this chapter.

Look at each of your staff members and ask yourself: Are they clear about the big picture? Do they understand their work the same way you do? If the answer is 'no' for any of them, then you need to find an opportunity to share with them the way that you see your department running. You can do this in a formal setting or you can have an informal chat, but the key is to communicate with them.

The next thing you need to do is monitor the way that you give instructions. When you talk to people, I want to assure you, there is bound to be some miscommunication and the reason for the miscommunication is primarily because you are human and they are human. To develop your communication skills, you need to identify situations where there is a breakdown in communication. You gave an instruction and the person got it wrong. You cannot possibly manage other human beings if they do not know what you want – and remember, it is your responsibility to make this clear.

If you don't have any miscommunications, it is not because you are a perfect communicator; it is probably because you didn't notice them. Everybody communicates poorly some of the time.

Try to find solutions to those breakdowns by using the CRIS model. When you do this, it is important for you to identify which part of CRIS was the cause of the breakdown. Was it a failure to check for clarity of communication? Was it the reporting structure? Was it because you didn't involve the person? Or was it because you did not set standards?

Being clear is an essential component of effective management. The clearer you are in your own mind about what has to be done, and the clearer you make that to other people, the more effective a manager you are going to be.

Note

1. The terms power, authority and influence were first used by Ichak Adizes, *How to Solve the Mismanagement Crisis: Diagnosis and Treatment of Management Problems* (Adizes Institute, 1979).

2

Commitment

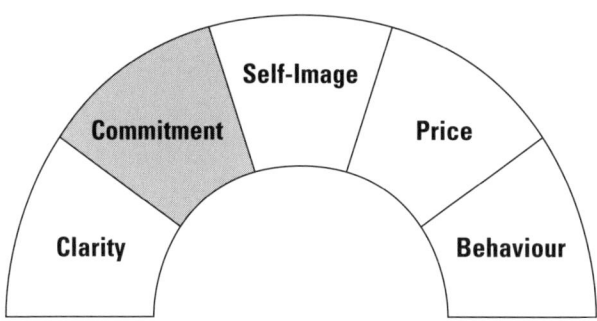

The second part of the arch is commitment. It is perfectly possible that a staff member knows exactly what you want them to do: your instruction was very clear. But still they do not do it. If clarity is not the problem, the next possible reason is quite simply that they lack commitment. If a person is not committed to what they have to do, they won't do it – or, if they do, they will do it reluctantly.

Commitment is not a 'nice to have'; it is absolutely essential in business. There is a vast difference in performance between someone who is passionately committed and someone who is not committed at all. A highly committed person will go out of their way to perform their tasks more accurately, faster and to a higher quality standard than somebody who is not committed at all. The person who is not committed thinks a job is a job. They say: I do as little work as I can possibly get away with, and I count the hours until I go home, and I count the days until the weekend and the weeks until my vacation.

Commitment operates on a variety of levels; one can be committed to the company, or to a manager, or to a particular task. You could have someone who is highly committed to the company but not to their manager because they have a bad relationship with her. Or you could have a person who is committed to the company but does not like the task that they are being asked to carry out. Whether the person lacks commitment to the company, the manager or the task, they are not going to get things done.

Can you just imagine how it would be if everyone was passionately committed to the company, to the manager and to the task? That would be absolute utopia. But this hardly ever happens, so we should not be surprised if we are not achieving it.

In this chapter I will show you how to take active steps to improve the levels of commitment that you have in the workplace, in order to get as close as you possibly can to utopia.

Let's look at the nature of commitment. Why are some people more committed than others?

WHAT'S IN IT FOR ME?

People are committed when they have good reasons for doing something. The more good reasons you have, the more committed you are going to be.

Here is an example. Your manager comes to you and says: 'I need you to do something very important for the company over the next month. We are flighting a series of ads in the newspaper, on TV and radio, to raise people's awareness of our company. We want to be sure that these ads are working, and we also want to know, at a very deep level, how our campaign is changing the impression people have of the company over a period of time. So we would like to see what people think at the beginning of the campaign, then in the middle, and then at the end.

'What I'm going to need you to do,' she says to you, 'is to go and do in-depth interviews with families, not with individuals – with whole families together – because we want to see what Mom and Dad and the kids think as a result of our efforts. These interviews will take you about an hour per family. We want you to interview at least three families every single night. We want you to do this seven nights a week, for the full four weeks that we are running this campaign. So we want you to work three to four hours every night, Monday through Sunday, for the next 30 days. Oh, and by the way, there is no budget for overtime.'

At this point, you will probably ask yourself the famous five-word question:

What's in it for me?

What's in it for me? What am I going to get out of this? Let's face it, if there is no reason for you to do it, why would you bother? Your manager has just told you that there is no money for overtime, so why does she think you would be remotely interested in spending every single night for the next month, Monday through Sunday, working for the company? There will be no socialising, there will be no television, and you won't see your children. Why do they think you'd be interested in doing that?

Human beings are driven by a psychological principle. We are all tuned in to a single radio station called WIIFM – *What's in it for me?* If there's a lot in it for me, if I have good reasons for doing something, I will be very committed. If there's not much in it for me, I won't. That is how human beings function. That is how you have been hard-wired.

Getting you to do this work seems hopeless, and probably is hopeless unless you understand another concept: hot buttons.

HOT BUTTONS

People are driven by what I call 'hot buttons'. By hot buttons I mean the five most important issues at this time in your life. People need and want hundreds of different things, from love to money, from religion to career. But we don't want them all with the same level of intensity. If we had to list them from the most important to the least important, there would have to be a top five. We call these top five your hot buttons. These are the most important issues in your life right now. Now, your hot buttons do change over time, as you grow and develop. It is possible for sport to be the most important thing in your life at 18, but at 35 your children might be the most important. But at any stage there is a top five. Knowing a person's hot buttons gives you a very useful tool with which to gain and stimulate their commitment.

Hot Buttons

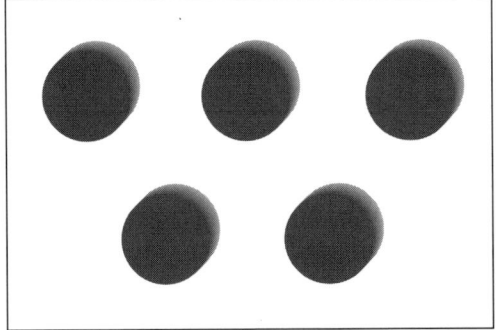

The five most important issues at this time in your life.

Hot buttons are generally non-tangible wants and needs such as love, respect, comfort, family, friendship and status. But they could as easily be a possession, an achievement or a challenge. They are the things that make a person tick.

People are very different. On the surface they might look similar, but the deeper we get, the more we are clearly able to see the differences that make people so interesting. These differences are a function of people having different hot buttons, different important issues in their lives at a particular time.

Now let's go back to our story about the advertising survey and analyse it in terms of hot buttons.

Like anyone else, you need and desire many things. Let's say you want to be loved, you like money, you like having fun, you like being appreciated, you like a challenge, you are thirsty for knowledge, you want to grow, and you care about your family. Career is very important to you, as is status. You are also a religious person, so your faith is important. You also like belonging to things. It is important for you to succeed. You spend a lot of time and energy on your friends and they are important to you. So is your home. And you love sport.

But of all these things (and, by the way, there might be hundreds of others), there are five that are most important to you right now – because of where you are in your career, because of your age, because of all sorts of things. There are five things that are most important out of this lot. You like money, you need money, you never have a great deal of it – you are always a little short. You love being challenged; that's just who you are. If somebody offers you a challenge, you take it. You are thirsty for knowledge; you want to know everything, all the time. Your career is very important to you right now. You are taking it enormously seriously and you are putting in a lot of effort. And status is important.

Hot buttons

○ Love	● **CAREER**
● **MONEY**	● **STATUS**
○ Fun	○ Faith
○ Appreciation	○ Belonging
● **CHALLENGE**	○ Success
● **KNOWLEDGE**	○ Friends
○ Growth	○ Home
○ Family	○ Sport

Out of all your needs and desires, your hot buttons are money, challenge, knowledge, career and status. Your manager tells you that there will be no overtime pay for the advertising survey; that is not good news. But then she says: 'You must understand that this work is extremely challenging; nobody has ever followed up a marketing campaign in this way. To do it correctly will not be easy, but we believe you really can.' She has just hit a hot button – challenge.

Then she says to you: 'By the time you have finished the month you will have learnt an enormous amount about the effects of advertising on families and individuals. You will learn more about branding, positioning and advertising than you could learn in a year-long course.' She has just hit a second hot button – knowledge.

Then she says: 'You must understand that when you put this report together, it will be known as the Smith Report; it will have your name on the front. When we talk about it, it will be the Smith Report that everybody is referring to. This will obviously be circulated among all the GMs, and among all the Board Members.' She has just hit another hot button – the need for status.

Then she looks at you and says: 'At the meeting of the Board of Directors, which is coming up in two months' time, you will be required to talk to them about your report and what you found. And as I'm sure you understand, that won't be bad for your career.' She has just hit another hot button – career. She has hit four out of five of your hot buttons, your most important needs. You would probably be prepared to do anything to make this happen. You'd be prepared to walk barefoot over broken glass, because your hot buttons are being pressed. People are committed to their work, to a task, to an institution or to a person, to the degree that that task, person, institution – or whatever – hits a hot button, and obviously the more hot buttons, the more commitment. Commitment is a function of hot buttons. That's how it works.

To see this point more clearly, let's imagine a different person, with different hot buttons, being asked to take part in the advertising survey. Of all the things that this person wants – love, money, fun, career, status, and so on – the most important are money, family, faith, friends and sport. These are his hot buttons. Now his manager comes to him and asks him to take part in the advertising survey, three hours every night for the next month, for no extra pay.

Hot buttons

◉ Love	◉ Career
● **MONEY**	◉ Status
◉ Fun	● **FAITH**
◉ Appreciation	◉ Belonging
◉ Challenge	◉ Success
◉ Knowledge	● **FRIENDS**
◉ Growth	◉ Home
● **FAMILY**	● **SPORT**

Look at his hot buttons. There is nothing that the manager could say to him to make him excited about doing this project. Challenge doesn't interest him, knowledge doesn't interest him, career is not that important, nor is status. What is important to him is family. He wants to be with his family every night, or as often as he possibly can. He attends church services on a Sunday evening and has a Bible study group during the week, and he certainly doesn't want to sacrifice that: his faith is too important. He likes spending evenings with his friends. He's obsessed with sport, and he doesn't want to miss out on all the sport on TV or his squash game every Wednesday night. So, when the manager asks him if he'll take the project on, he'll probably say: 'I really would like to, but I can't. I lead a Bible study group once a week and they rely on me, and I'm part of the choir on a Sunday night. I'm part of a league and I play sport every Wednesday night. Thanks so much for asking me; I do appreciate your interest in me.'

The person is not committed because the task is of no interest to him and doesn't touch any hot buttons. The only way the manager could possibly get him to do it would be to say, 'You do understand that we would consider your inability to help us here when we look at your bonus.' Now that might possibly touch his feeling about money, but he might think to himself: 'The difference in my bonus will be so little because I didn't do this project, especially if I can persuade them that I really can't, even if I want to.' It's not enough to make him really committed. His other hot buttons, the four other ones, will be too strong to make that hot button effective.

IDENTIFYING PEOPLE'S HOT BUTTONS

As a manager you need to motivate people, to get them committed. To do this you have to learn to understand human beings, to know what makes them tick, and the way that you start this process is by getting to know your staff. You need to study them, and ask yourself: 'What are their hot buttons? What seems to matter to this person?' By observing, you will become an astute student of human beings. And by becoming an astute student of human beings, you will become an even better manager. But don't make the mistake of thinking this is easy – it isn't; it requires effort and attention.

I am going to describe a person, and as I do, try to identify his five hot buttons. The man is a medical specialist and he has a beautiful suite of rooms in an upmarket suburb, magnificently furnished, with original artworks on the walls. He wears beautiful and expensive clothes and is always very well groomed. He drives a silver-grey convertible Porsche – the latest model. You get the picture? If I asked you what his hot buttons are, you would probably say material goods, appearances, status, wealth and image.

Now let me tell you a little more about him. He has a son with Down's syndrome and he spends a lot of his time working for the school for children with special needs where his son is a pupil. He is an active member of the Parents' Association, and he also donates a lot of his own money to the school. Every evening, on his way home, he passes his mother's flat and has a drink with her; he has been doing this every night since his father died, because he believes she might be lonely and needs to know that there are people there for her. A number of years ago his wife had a minor psychological breakdown, and ever since then he has told his nurse that if she ever phones, no matter whom he is with, she must be put through immediately.

Given this new information, you would no longer say that his hot buttons are material goods, status, wealth and the like, but that they include family, community, loyalty and charity.

You see, when we looked at the man superficially, we had a very quick and easy sense of what he was about. There is a trap in using hot buttons, and the trap is that we can use them very superficially, applying them to people quickly and thoughtlessly, without looking deeper at them. Most people jump to quick, and often silly, conclusions about other people. They also make generalisations, which are almost always incorrect.

Talk to your staff, listen to your staff, observe your staff, and then try to work out their hot buttons. Over time you will probably have to revise them. Sometimes, of course, you get it right first time. This might mean that you are very intuitive – or maybe just plain lucky. But our ability to use hot buttons tends to grow with experience, and we get sharper and sharper at identifying them.

You can work out people's hot buttons by observing how they behave – the way they work, how they talk, how they dress, what they are interested in, all sorts of information you know about the person. Or you could ask them questions, such as: What gives you deep satisfaction in your work? What do you dislike most in your work? What is the most important thing for you in your work? What do you want to achieve from your career? If you could pick your ideal job what would it be? Outside of work what is your favourite pastime?

And let's not forget an important point. Ask *yourself* these questions – to work out your own hot buttons. This is quite a difficult thing to do, but it will give you insight into what motivates you.

People generally don't know that hot buttons exist, and as a result they don't try to hide them. If you look at people carefully, you will find out how easy it is to see their hot buttons.

USING HOT BUTTONS

As you analyse hot buttons you will probably find yourself getting clearer insight into why people do what they do, and why they are like they are. You can predict how they will react to certain situations, and you can use that knowledge next time when you need to motivate them. Remember that people will not be committed to doing something unless it has some relationship to their hot buttons.

There is one issue, though, that we need to talk about when we deal with hot buttons, and that is the issue of manipulation.

Manipulate:

Control or influence (a person or situation) cleverly, unfairly, or unscrupulously: *the masses were deceived and manipulated by a tiny group.*

The New Oxford Dictionary of English

The word 'manipulate', according to the *New Oxford Dictionary of English*, means to control or influence a person or situation cleverly, unfairly or unscrupulously. An example of how you would use this in a sentence is: 'The masses were deceived and manipulated by a tiny group.' When you manipulate somebody, you are doing something unfair and unscrupulous. If you manipulate them into agreeing to do something, and they find out what you have done, they will be very sorry that they agreed.

Using hot buttons is very different from manipulation. If you use hot buttons, and the person finds out what you have done, they will be as pleased to have agreed as if they hadn't found out. All we are doing with hot buttons is connecting what the person wants anyway to the situation that they are in. Remember I said in the last chapter that the most important way in which managers control the behaviour of their staff is influence. Influence is the ability to get someone to want to do what you want them to do. That's exactly what you do when you link someone's work to their hot buttons.

The job of the manager is to try to connect the person's work to their hot buttons. The more hot buttons you can touch, the more dedicated the person will be to their work. If you can't relate their work to their hot buttons, you will probably have a great deal of difficulty in motivating them. It is unfortunate, but it is a fact. You need to learn how to identify people's hot buttons and then see how you can link them to their work, even if it is not a direct link.

For example, Kevin works in a supermarket; his hot buttons are respect, people contact, career, money and fun. Knowing that his hot buttons are career and money, you talk to him about what it takes to get ahead in the company – what he must do to become the kind of person who will be promoted. If he is promoted he will be able to earn more money, which addresses that hot button. He also values respect, so you talk to him about how giving respect is what earns respect, how if you show people respect they will respond to you with the same sort of respect. You might even talk to him about how he can make his job more fun by giving himself challenges in terms of the appearance of his work area, or the speed at which he serves, or with little competitions with himself about how many conversations he can have with people who come to his scale.

Once you have identified the hot buttons of the people who work for you, you can do a similar exercise, linking their hot buttons to the work they have to do. Think about what you could and should do differently with your staff, in order to gain their commitment. If your staff are committed, they will get more of the right things done.

3

Self-Image

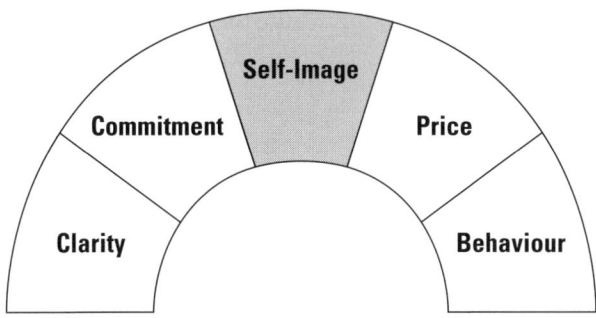

The third part of the arch is self-image. The reason I have placed self-image at the centre of the arch is because your self-image is absolutely central to your performance and success – in business and in life in general. Knowing about self-image will also give you the ability to deal with other people and assist them in their growth and development.

SELF-IMAGE PSYCHOLOGY

If you were managing computers it really wouldn't matter whether or not you were any good at dealing with people. But as a manager of human beings you have to become an amateur psychologist. You have to know how to deal with people, how to get the most out of them, and, of course, how to get the most out of yourself.

There are countless theories of psychology, but the theory I will use here is called self-image psychology. Self-image psychologists hold that the single most important factor that determines how you function is your self-image. More than anything else, it will determine how high you go in your career, and in fact how successful you are in all aspects of your life.

Human beings have between 200 and 300 self-images. You have a self-image of yourself as a friend, as a husband or wife, as a parent, as an employee, as a manager, as a sports person, as a driver. You have a self-image of your intelligence, your attractiveness and the way you dress. You have hundreds and hundreds of self-images. A self-image is a picture of yourself in your mind. The important thing about the self-image is that we always live up to it. It doesn't matter if it is high or low; you always live up to your self-image.

This point is perhaps best illustrated by one of the earliest writers of self-image psychology, Maxwell Maltz, who published the book *Psycho-Cybernetics* in 1960. Maxwell Maltz was a plastic surgeon who did cosmetic surgery to improve people's looks. On one occasion, a woman with a very pronounced hooked nose came to him, to have her nose recreated. When he removed the bandages after the operation, he was very satisfied with the result: she looked absolutely gorgeous. But when she looked in the mirror she said: 'Doctor, I don't see much difference, I still feel ugly.' Her self-image was so powerful that it reinterpreted the way she saw herself in the mirror. Maxwell Maltz experienced reactions like this again and again, and this led him to understand the centrality of the self-image.

Your self-image is a deep belief about yourself. It is who you believe you really are. It is different from a wish. There are many things you might wish that you could be or do, but these are different from the things you know you are and can do. The self-image always relates to those things we know about ourselves.

People always perform in accordance with their self-image. In fact, we are not capable of performing any other way for an extended period of time. People will always perform more or less in accordance with their deep beliefs about themselves.

Let's examine the mechanism that lies behind the self-image, because the more we understand this mechanism, the more easily we will be able to do something with it. When your self-image and your performance are on exactly the same level, we talk of being in your 'comfort zone'. Your comfort zone is the point at which you feel comfortable about the way things are. If your self-image is high and your performance is good, you'll be satisfied with your performance. If your self-image is low and your performance is poor, you'll also be satisfied. In both cases you'll be in a comfort zone. If you perform above or below your self-image, you will experience discomfort, and you'll take corrective action to bring your performance back in line with your self-image.

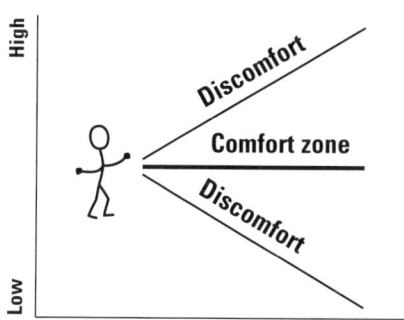

Let's say, for example, that you consider yourself to be an excellent cook. One night, when your guests arrive for dinner, everything goes wrong. The soup is too salty, the main course is burnt, and even your famous lemon meringue pie looks more like a fried egg. Even though your guests are very polite, you feel devastated. The evening has been an utter disaster. Your self-image as a cook is very high, and because your performance was low, you feel discomfort, in the form of embarrassment or failure.

So what do you do? The next time you invite people round for dinner, you start preparing the meal hours before and you take particular care over every detail. You cook an amazing meal and your guests tell you so. 'Thank you very much,' you say – and you think to yourself: *Yes! I did it!*

Let's look at what happened here. After the first meal, you felt discomfort, because your performance was lower than your self-image. So you took self-correcting action to push your performance up, in line with your self-image, to get back into your comfort zone. You were internally driven by your self-image saying: *That's not me; I'm better than that.*

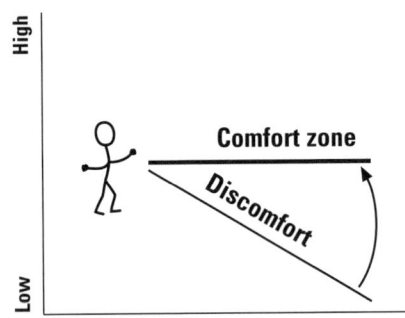

Now, let's imagine that – unlike the example above – you don't see yourself as a good cook at all. Your idea of cooking is popping bread in the toaster and pre-prepared meals in the microwave – and even that can be a bit of a challenge. A few colleagues are at your house one Saturday doing some work, and one of them says: 'Can we get something to eat? I'm starving.' You say that you're not any good at cooking but you've got something in the freezer. You put it in the microwave, but for too long, and it tastes awful – and your guests tell you so. You'll probably say to them: 'I told you so.' Cooking just isn't your thing. Your performance is bad, and you're used to that. It's in line with your low self-image as a cook. And if you have the same colleagues round a week later, you won't do anything differently, because you're comfortable with your performance.

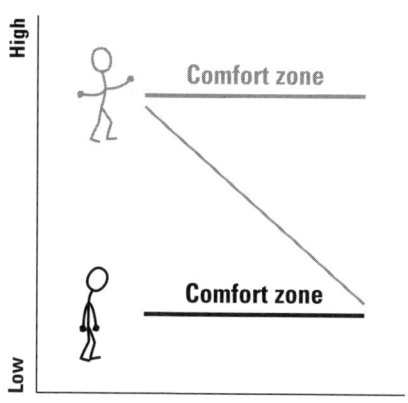

You can see why this has huge application in the work context. If somebody with a low self-image performs badly, they will be highly unlikely to do anything about it. But if their self-image is higher than their performance, they will feel discomfort, and that discomfort will propel them to take corrective action, to push their performance back to where it really should be. Your self-image drives your actions and your aspirations, provided it is high enough. So if, for example, you see yourself as a manager who treats staff fairly, and you are unreasonably critical of one of them, you'll take corrective action and improve your performance.

The same applies when you exceed your self-image. If your performance is higher than your self-image, you will also feel discomfort. You will have a feeling that this isn't you, that it can't last, that you will never keep it up. You don't perform at that high a level. If you did, it was a fluke; you got lucky and it is unlikely to repeat itself. And because you have those feelings, you will, without knowing it, drop your performance until you get back into your comfort zone. That is how human beings are designed; that's how we function. We cannot function in any other way.

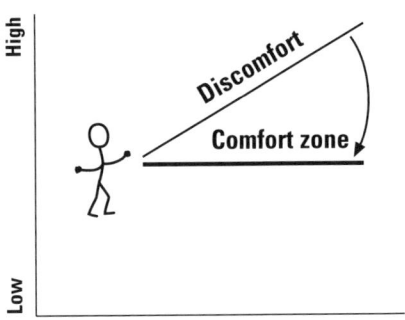

In a relationship, for example, you'll not only feel discomfort if you behave discourteously to your partner, in a way that you see as unacceptable, but also if you act in a way that is more courteous and chivalrous than you think you need to. It doesn't feel a hundred per cent natural; you know that you are trying too hard. You feel a mild discomfort about the effort you made to behave like that, so you revert to what you believe is your normal level of behaviour and you drop your performance to get back into your comfort zone.

It's okay to have a low self-image in some areas. Most of us will not be upset that we aren't excellent Sumo wrestlers who weigh hundreds of kilograms. Your self-image as a Sumo wrestler is very low indeed, and you're comfortable with that. Your self-image is: 'I'm not a Sumo wrestler and I don't want to be a Sumo wrestler.'

At the same time, people have an average, overall self-image. That's the general way you think about yourself. People who generally feel better about themselves succeed more often than people who don't. Having a good, solid, healthy self-image is an essential component of mental health and personal, social and business success. It is very difficult to function as a good manager if you have a low self-image.

RAISING YOUR SELF-IMAGE

If you have a low self-image, you need to raise it to where you think it should be, so that your performance can follow. Your performance will always follow your self-image. If your self-image is low and you simply try as hard as you can to improve your performance, you will always fall back to the level of your self-image. As Henry Ford said, if you believe you can do something, or if you believe you can't, you are right in both cases.

The only way you will be able to push up your performance with long-lasting effects is by raising your self-image. If you look at areas in your life where you tried to perform better, but didn't, and reverted back to your previous level of performance, this was almost always because you didn't raise your self-image at the same time. If you are desperate to improve your performance, at least see to it that you are improving your self-image at the same time.

Your self-image takes a long time to improve, but there is something you can do about it. Your mind doesn't know the difference between reality and fantasy, as you know from watching suspenseful movies. You start feeling tense and afraid, because you can see the murderer lurking in the dark passage as the woman opens the front door. As he whips a piece of piano wire around her neck, your body goes tense and you are petrified.

Now, you know that these events didn't happen. You know this is just a movie. You know the woman is not dead; she's just an actress, and you've seen her in another, more recent, film. And yet your body reacts as if it was real. You feel tension, fear and anxiety. Your mind cannot tell the difference between reality and fantasy. This is, in fact, very good news, because if our self-image is not appropriate, we can change it by simply visualising – picturing how we would like to be – over and over again.

Let me tell you that every high-performing sports person uses this technique regularly and often. Jack Nicklaus said he never moved his golf club without picturing himself with the perfect swing, the perfect trajectory and the perfect landing. Gary Player, too, is an obsessive visualiser. He says that when he plays a bad shot he immediately visualises himself playing that same shot perfectly so that he imprints it on his brain. Years before he won the British Open, before he even *entered* it, Gary Player rehearsed the speech that he would make on winning that tournament. In his mind he was building up a self-image of Gary Player, the man who won the British Open, years before he did. Once his self-image was there, it was possible for him to raise his performance to make that happen.

How do you visualise? Relax in a comfortable place, close your eyes, and picture yourself as you want to be. For example, see yourself as confident, self-disciplined, caring towards your staff, knowledgeable about your work, and so on. Picture yourself succeeding at what you do. You are the expert. You are highly competent. See yourself like that. Picture yourself interacting with other people, doing things that you are able to do now that you have got the self-image. Don't let any negative ideas in. While you are doing this visualisation there might be a temptation for you to say: 'Yes, but that won't happen for me.' Don't do that. Avoid that, because all this information is being imprinted on your brain and the last thing you want to do is imprint the wrong information on your brain.

Picture yourself performing well as often as you possibly can. The more often you do this, the more you imprint it on your brain. Most people who don't realise how their minds work think about themselves failing all the time, and that is why they bring failure into their reality.

The self-image is at the centre of your arch, because it is the single most important thing that is going to determine what you actually achieve. Obviously you can't achieve anything unless you are clear about what you want to achieve, and you won't bother trying to do anything about it unless you are committed. But you won't be *able* to do it unless your self-image is appropriate to what you want to achieve.

We'll get back to self-image later in the chapter, in relation to your staff, but now we are ready to look at another issue, the issue of ego states.

EGO STATES

An ego state is how you feel about yourself and the world at a particular moment. Unlike the self-image, which changes very slowly, ego states are current and immediate and change quickly.

Human beings function out of three ego states: 'parent', 'adult' and 'child'. When we are in parent mode we are in command and in control, we are protective, judgmental and disciplining. When we are in child mode, we're fun-loving, spontaneous, irresponsible and emotional. When we're in adult mode we are logical, disciplined, unemotional, rational, confident and clear thinking.

Of course, you don't have to be a parent to be in a 'parent' ego state; you don't have to be a child to be in 'child'; you don't even have to be an adult to be in 'adult' mode. A man taking care of his 85-year-old mother is often in parent mode and the mother is in child mode. Husbands and wives, too, often shift between parent and child roles with one another. When the wife can't get the car to start, the husband might say, 'Don't you worry about this; I'll take care of it.' He is acting like a parent. Or the wife could order her husband around in the kitchen, saying: 'Don't touch that, put that here, do this,' and so on. Then she is acting like a parent.

Normal human beings flip in and out of these states – from child to adult to parent – and they flip in and out very quickly. If a person always behaves towards other people in parent mode – always looking after them, telling them what to do, always thoroughly controlling everybody – he or she might have a problem. If somebody is stuck in child mode – irresponsible, fun-loving, emotional and uncontrolled all the time – he or she also has a problem. So does somebody who is always in adult mode – someone who is always controlled, who never laughs with abandon, who never has fun, who is always holding in. And that kind of person is very boring.

Each of these states has an appropriate place: there are times when it is thoroughly appropriate to be parent, adult or child. For example, it is entirely appropriate to act like a child when watching sport on a Saturday afternoon. You get excited, yell at the ref, and have fun. And if you invited someone over to join you, you'd probably want them to act the same way. The last thing you'd want is someone in a parent or adult state.

In the world of work, you seldom want people to act like children. Imagine a production director walking down the factory floor and seeing six employees standing with their arms folded, around a machine that is not operating. He greets the workers pleasantly, asks them what is going on, and they tell him that the machine is not working.

'How long has this machine not been working?' he asks.

'It's not been working for one-and-a-half hours,' they reply.

'I see,' says the production director, 'so six people have been standing around, each for one-and-a-half hours – the equivalent of nine working hours, more than one full day's work – doing absolutely nothing.'

'That's right,' they say.

'And what are you waiting for?' asks the production director.

'Well,' they say, 'we're waiting for a mechanic.'

'Oh,' he says, 'that's a relief.'

And then he thinks for a moment and says, 'Have you called a mechanic?'

'No,' they say.

So he says, 'Then what are you waiting for?'

'We're waiting for the supervisor,' they say.

'And what will the supervisor do?' he asks.

'Well,' they say, 'the supervisor will call the mechanic.'

He can't believe his ears. The people are standing round doing absolutely nothing because they took no initiative.

The workers are in a child ego state. Children don't take initiative, children don't take responsibility, children don't take charge – they wait for an adult to take control of them. You can be sure that if one of the workers went home and found that there was no dinner because the stove was broken, he would shift into adult mode and take care of that situation far more quickly.

As manager, at work, it is absolutely essential that you are in adult ego state all the time. There are occasions – when you go away on a seminar or a conference, for example – when you can revert to child after hours. But for the world of work, as a manager, you will be required to be in an adult ego state. When you feel adult, you think clearly and behave well. It is the only ego state that you can count on as being the correct one. It is very difficult to function as an effective manager if you're not in adult mode.

When you're in the presence of someone whom you respect highly – the CEO of a large corporation, for example – you need to relate to them as an adult. Many people make the mistake of shifting into child mode. But when you're in child mode you don't think clearly and you don't give a good account of yourself. You need to remain in adult mode. This doesn't mean that you slap the person on the back and say: 'Hey, my man!' You don't have to be overfamiliar. You need to behave like an adult who is in the presence of another, highly intelligent and accomplished adult. There are two adults in the room, and you as an adult are appreciating the remarkable achievements of the other.

It is equally important that managers avoid the parent ego state, when relating to their staff. A lot of bad managers think they should relate to their staff that way. This was the ego state of the old-fashioned manager for many, many years. What these managers are unaware of is that this pushes the staff member into child mode, and then you are not going to get much out of them.

This is how ego states work. Whenever you are in a parent ego state, you are probably going to push the other person into child mode. And when you are in child mode you will usually push the other person into parent mode. When you are in adult mode you are usually going to make the other person feel adult too.

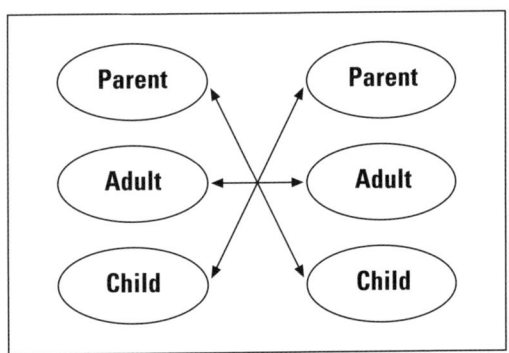

If you act like a parent with your staff, you will force them into child mode. You could have the wounded child, when they feel weak and vulnerable, humiliated and upset, or the rebellious child, when they start arguing back and getting cheeky and resist what they are being told. You are paying an adult's wage and getting a child – someone who doesn't think clearly, doesn't take initiative and doesn't make the right things happen. It is very, very important that you never allow your staff to slip into child mode. When your staff are in adult mode they are responsible, they are proactive and they are diligent.

Managers must be particularly careful when they speak a language that is not a staff member's first language. If you don't speak a language well, you often feel insecure and inferior – like a child. This is very important in multilingual countries like South Africa, where the language used most in business is English, but staff could speak one of many other languages. When we speak to them in English we are speaking in their second or third language. This could have a terrible effect, because we tend to talk down to them, as if they are inferior, as if they are stupid. So we come across as parent, and we push them down to child.

If you are talking to someone who is speaking to you in their second or third language, it is important to remind yourself that he or she is an intelligent adult who is not fully proficient in your language. They are not stupid; they just don't understand well. If you can remind yourself that you are talking to an intelligent adult, you will make them feel like an adult and you will get an adult's work out of them. The manager who forgets this will never get as much as he or she possibly can out of his or her staff members.

There is another problem that comes up very often, and it is a function of cultural differences. It appears mainly among well-brought-up, rural people, who have been taught to be polite and respectful to their elders. As a result they often make the mistake of thinking that if they are in the company of somebody who is older than them, or who is their superior, they must go into a child ego state. As we've seen, this is a mistake, because the child ego state is not appropriate for the world of work.

YOUR STAFF'S SELF-IMAGE

Armed with this information on self-image and ego states, you can get more out of your staff. Remember, you are not a psychologist, and you are not going to do therapy on your staff. But some knowledge of psychology is essential for dealing with people, and management is all about people.

The first thing to note – and this is very important – is that you must do everything you can to assist your staff to have a better self-image. People who have a good self-image perform better than people who have a poor self-image. There are some managers who try to knock their staff, put them down all the time, and make them feel inferior. Whenever you do this you are damaging the person's self-image and in the long run (and possibly even in the short run), you are going to get poor performance out of them. The greatest gift that managers can give their staff is a good self-image – letting them believe in themselves, by seeing that you believe in them. We must be careful that we always relate to people in such a way that we enhance their self-image and not destroy it.

Now, having said that, what do you do when a staff member has an inflated self-image, when they are out of touch with their performance levels and think they are better than they really are?

Let's say a certain staff member has the following self-image: she sees herself as clever, slightly lacking in confidence, liked by others, excellent at her job and eager. When you look at her performance, you think her self-image is inflated in two areas. She thinks she is clever, but you think she is above average but nothing special. She thinks she is excellent at her job, but you think she is not performing.

Staff member's self-image

1. ~~Clever~~   *above average, nothing special*
2. **Lacking confidence**
3. **Liked by others**
4. ~~Excellent at my job~~   *not performing*
5 **Eager**

Would it be useful for you to correct her perception of herself as clever? Would it be useful to tell her that she is above average but nothing special? What would happen? If you managed to persuade her that she is nothing special, would you be motivating her, or demotivating her? Would it increase her performance, or decrease it?

It is always better for somebody to think well of themselves than to think poorly. If they think they are clever, they are more likely to behave like a clever person than if they think they are limited. You would wish people to have a better self-image than they currently have, provided, of course, that it is not completely inflated. In this case the person thinks she is clever, but she is not. There will be no value in trying to change her self-image in this regard.

Let's have a look at her self-image as someone who is excellent at her work. When you look at her you see somebody who is not performing. How is it possible that somebody who is not performing believes they're excellent? Most managers who do not understand self-image psychology will usually blame the person and say: 'This person is out of touch with reality.' The professional manager who understands concepts like self-image will see a big red light going on, and the red light says: 'There is something very wrong with the way that this person has been managed. How is it possible that they believe they are excellent at their job when they are not performing?'

As a trainer I have heard this from countless people: 'My staff think they are much better than they are, and they really aren't performing.' The question I always ask them is: 'How long have you been managing this person?' And every now and then the answer is two years, three years or five years. How is it possible that in five years, or two years, or even one year, they didn't know that they were not performing? The manager has obviously failed the staff member. He or she has failed to give the person adequate feedback that makes them confront the reality of their work. If you failed to give appropriate feedback at their development review, if you didn't want to give it to them 'in the face', you haven't allowed them to face the truth; you can hardly blame them for believing that they are excellent when they are not performing. Whenever you have somebody with an inflated image of their performance, you have somebody who has been poorly handled by a manager for far too long.

I would suggest that most managers who do not confront the non-performance of their staff do so because, somehow or other, they feel like a child towards the staff member. If they felt like an adult they would approach the issue intelligently and constructively. The last thing you want to do is come across as a parent, because then you would turn the other person into a child. If you have to confront the other person's non-performance, you must confront them as an adult and allow them to feel like an adult too. Children don't do anything; they don't take initiative and they don't correct their behaviour. Only adults do that, and that is why you must make your staff feel adult all the time.

SELF-IMAGE AND TASKS

Let's recap how the self-image works. We said that your self-image controls your performance and your self-image always wants you to be in your comfort zone. So if you ever perform above your self-image, you will say to yourself that this is too good to be true, this can't last, and without even knowing it you will drop your performance to get back into your comfort zone. If, on the other hand, you perform below your self-image, you will be ashamed or angry; you will feel some form of discomfort, and that will drive you towards improving your performance until you get back into your comfort zone.

That drive is an inner drive, a built-in drive; it is the way that your mind works; it is the way human beings have been programmed. You will always function like that. You will always perform according to your self-image and you will always move towards your comfort zone. Perform above your self-image and you will drop your performance, perform below and you will raise it.

This has significant implications for the kind of work that we give to people. You always want to match a person's tasks to their self-image. It takes far too long to change a person's self-image, and for that reason you're almost always better off giving people tasks that are in keeping with their self-image. Very often we give tasks to staff that are too overwhelming or too menial for them. If the task is beneath their self-image they will be disinclined to do it. If the task is above their self-image they will struggle with it, they will feel uncomfortable, and at the end of the day they will not do it or not do it properly.

You need to look at the specific tasks that your staff do, and identify whether their self-image for the task is high or low, and what ego state they are usually in when they do it. Bear in mind that the self-image and ego states always relate to a specific task, that somebody can have a very weak self-image about one thing and a very strong self-image about another. Somebody can be in a child ego state when they do one activity, and in parent or adult mode when they do another. So we always have to relate this back to the task.

You could have a staff member who has a low self-image when dealing with customers; he feels unsure of himself and out of control. He is in a child ego state. When he does paperwork, on the other hand, his self-image is high and he's in an adult ego state. He knows what to do, he can defend himself to anyone on what he has done and why. No one can catch him out with inaccuracies or mistakes.

The more you look for self-image and ego states in action, the more easily you will be able to spot them. People don't know that you are looking for these things and they don't think of hiding them, so they are relatively easy to see if you apply your mind. You need to allocate work to people whose self-image allows them to do it, and whose ego state is appropriate to the task.

In summary, we should be very careful to boost people's self-image rather than bash it, and we should be careful to relate to them as an adult so that they will relate to us as adults. People who feel adult are in control, think better and work better. Adult is the most appropriate ego state at work.

Your staff's self-image is crucial to the type of work you can give them. No one will succeed at doing work that is above their self-image, or for that matter below their self-image. If they do the work, it will never be of a high quality. If you match your staff's work to their self-image, you will get better performance from them.

4

Price

The arch is an analytical tool that will increase your ability to understand what is going on in the managerial context. Armed with this knowledge, management takes on a whole new look. As opposed to being an unmanageable and confusing task, without any solution, it turns into a demanding task that has clearly identifiable problems and clearly identifiable solutions.

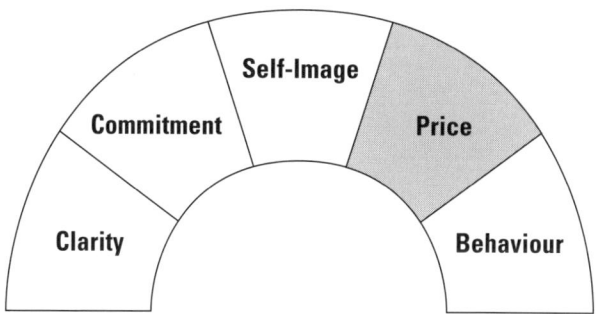

The fourth part of the arch is price. If you are sure that a problem is not related to clarity, commitment or self-image, then it could be related to price.

What do we mean by 'price'? Price is what a person has to suffer, sacrifice or give up in order to get the job done. Everything in life comes with a price. The price, in this context, is not necessarily money. When you want to buy something, you have to give up your money; in the same way, with everything in life, you have to give things up in order to get what you want.

For instance, if you want to study further, you will have to give up watching TV at night, so that you can do your studying. If you want to get fit, you have to give up sleeping late in the morning, so that you can run or go to gym at half past five. If you want to develop a relationship with your partner, you have to give up other things, like spending all your time with friends or playing the field.

Just being a manager comes with a price. As a manager you have to work hard. You have to put in the hours and be seen to be putting in the hours, and you have to take responsibility for the work of others. You have to set an example for your staff, so you must be careful about your own conduct. If you are late, discourteous, unreliable or unprofessional, you'll have a hard time getting staff to be punctual, courteous, reliable or professional. All of these things are prices that you have to pay in order to be a manager.

Price is the most important issue when it comes to staff. Very often the reason people do not perform well is quite simply because the price is too high. Now, it is the manager's duty to try to get maximum performance out of his or her staff – that's obvious. All too often managers forget to consider this vital aspect called price and therefore they only get a fraction of the real potential that people have.

There are three kinds of price: situational, emotional and preference. Let me give you an example to explain these.

Grace has been working at a supermarket for the past two years as a part-time employee. On Tuesdays and on Saturdays, she works as a bag packer at the till. She has often said how much she would like a permanent job, with all the perks that come with it – medical aid, pension and a housing loan. The store manager offers her full-time employment, as an assistant in the fish department. But she shows some hesitation; in fact she doesn't even look excited at the prospect! The manager is very surprised at this; he thought she would be delighted!

If we want to understand why Grace isn't delighted, we need to consider the three prices she might have to pay: situational, emotional and preference.

What is the situational price? Because of her family situation, she has to leave her one-year-old child in the care of a child-minder in the neighbourhood. Working at the store means long hours, and on top of that there's an hour-long journey to and from work. This would mean that Mondays to Fridays, and even to some extent on Saturdays, she would not see her child while he is awake. While she needs the job because she needs the money, the situation is quite difficult. She would need to find someone that she trusts enough to look after her child every day of the week. That is purely situational.

There might also be an emotional price she has to pay. She has always felt very comfortable with the cashiers that she has worked with, but the people who work in the fish department make her feel uncomfortable. She feels uneasy with them. She doesn't get on with them and she doesn't think they like her. If she took the job in the fish shop, she would have an emotional price to pay. The price would be to feel uncomfortable every day at work – spending eight hours with these people in order to have the job.

There might also be a price that is just a preference. Perhaps she doesn't like fish – she doesn't like the smell of fish, and she certainly doesn't like the idea of touching fish. She would prefer to work as a cashier or in the bakery or the deli. In taking the job she would have to pay the price of working with fish even though she prefers not to.

Any one of these might be the price Grace has to pay. The categories don't matter very much; I'm simply pointing out that the price comes in lots of different forms. In the workplace, as in all areas of life, there will be situational, emotional and preference prices to pay.

Once you have identified the price that you have to pay, you have to decide whether it is worth paying. If not, it is a good idea to stop doing whatever you're doing, put it on the back-burner, leave it for another time in your life, and move on. Let's say, for example, that you are given the opportunity to work in an overseas branch of your company for three months. This is an incredibly exciting opportunity – except that your wife is expecting your first child. If you go away for the three months you'll not be there for the birth of your child or even the first month of its life. The opportunity of working overseas comes with a price that is too high, one that you choose not to pay, so you turn down the offer.

Here's another example. In order to get ahead in your career, you need to study further. This would mean hours of study every day after work. That is a high price to pay. You enjoy relaxing at home, watching a bit of television, socialising with friends and going to see movies. If you want to get ahead, you are going to have to stop all that for six to eight months. During the week, every evening, you will simply have to put in the extra hours required to learn the new material.

You have to ask yourself whether the price is worth paying. Do the advantages outweigh the price that you have to pay? When you think of the promotional opportunities, higher income, increased knowledge and competence, you'd probably say that the six to eight months' inconvenience is really worth it. In that case, you go full steam ahead and you know what the price is. You are going full steam ahead with your eyes open, fully conscious of what this undertaking involves.

PAYMENT STRATEGY

Now we need to look at how to pay that price – your payment strategy. A payment strategy is a plan you put into action that forces you to do what you have to, when you have to do it, whether you like it or not.

> **A payment strategy is:**
>
> **a plan you put into action, that *forces* you to do what you have to do, when you have to do it, whether you like it or not!**

For example, if you decide to save some money every month, you will not have as much to spend on the luxuries that you enjoy. That is the price. But as the month goes on, you see a couple of things that you like, so you buy them, hoping that you'll still have some money left at the end of the month to put in your savings account. But, by the time the end of the month comes around, you have spent all your disposable income and saved nothing. Now you decide that you need a payment strategy that forces you to do what you have to do.

As a payment strategy you arrange a debit order on your bank account. What this means is that on the very day that your salary goes into your account, a fixed amount of money is taken off automatically, without anyone asking you whether you like it or not, and transferred into your savings account. Then you might see to it that the savings account is closed for six months or a year, which will prevent you from dipping into it every time you get the urge. You now have yourself a perfect payment strategy that will overcome the price you have to pay in order to build up your savings.

In order to be successful, you have to pay the price, and the problem with the price is that there are no discounts and you can't pay it off. The price of success always has to be paid in full and in advance. That is why we need to have a payment strategy, to ensure that we pay in full and in advance.

Bunker Hunt was one of America's most successful men. He was a self-made multi-billionaire and at his death in 1974 was the richest man in America. At the time he was earning one million dollars a week! What is remarkable about Bunker Hunt is that at age 37 he was a bankrupt farmer, and he made all his money after then.

Bunker Hunt was interviewed once on a radio station (which he happened to own), and the interviewer asked him about the secret of his success. Bunker Hunt answered that there are only two rules that you have to know and live by. First, you have to know exactly what it is that you want. If you don't know what you want you can't get it. That's the first rule. And the second rule is to work out the price that you are going to have to pay in order to achieve your goals and be prepared to pay the price.

Many people know what their goals are, and are sure of what the price is, but they are just not prepared to pay the price. We are human and because we are human we change our minds and aren't very good at keeping to the decisions we have made. Almost everyone has made New Year's resolutions and broken most of them by the third of January. It wasn't that you were insincere. It was quite simply that you didn't build in a payment strategy. A payment strategy forces you to stick to your goal and pay the price, even when you don't want to.

Bear in mind that you cannot reward *yourself* for doing the right thing. You might say: 'I'm going to exercise today and if I exercise today I'll give myself a chocolate.' Since you're the one who gives the chocolate and you are the one who exercises, wouldn't you agree that you can give the chocolate to yourself even if you don't exercise? If you are in control of the prize, you can award it to yourself whether you deserve it or not. So a good payment strategy is something that is external to you, because that way you are forced to pay the price whether you like it or not.

Finding appropriate payment strategies is often very difficult. But you must understand that it doesn't matter how hard it is and how much time it takes; you have to find a payment strategy. If you don't have a payment strategy you will not succeed in doing what you have to do, and the reason for this is that you are human.

A good payment strategy will ensure that you pay the price even when you don't feel like it. Many people know very clearly what they want. They might even be committed, and their self-image could be appropriate, but they are simply not prepared to pay the price that is required – or, if they are prepared, they never put a payment strategy into place and so they never pay the price and never achieve.

If you want to get fit, you might say: 'I need to get fit; I am perfectly clear. I am committed to getting fit, so I can fit into my clothes again. My self-image is of a thin person who is fit.' But in order to get fit, you have to run every morning. When the alarm goes off at 5:30 for your run, and it is cold or raining or you are tired, you simply roll over and continue sleeping. You have not paid the price. You need a payment strategy. So you arrange with other people that you will run with them and that they will pass your home and pick you up. That way you are sure that even if you feel tired and don't feel like doing it, you will find yourself getting out of bed, going outside and running with them, because they are waiting for you.

I know of a manager who did a similar thing with his staff. He knew he should be meeting with them one on one at least every second week, but he seldom did, because something more urgent always came up, and by year-end he had had very few one-on-one meetings. His payment strategy was to put the monkey on their shoulders and he told them that a part of their bonus was dependent on them having two one-on-one meetings with him per month. Now if he cancelled, they hounded him until they found a time to meet.

HELPING OTHER PEOPLE PAY THE PRICE

Having looked at the price you're paying and the payment strategy you can adopt to pay this price, we are now ready to look at the price that other people pay. We need to consider the price our staff are paying to do what we ask them to do. Not only because it is the right thing to do, not only because it is moral to be concerned about other people, but also because it makes good business sense. The manager who does not take into account the price that staff are paying will find that he or she gets less work done than the manager who does take the price into account.

But at the same time, we're not looking at the price our staff are paying in order to excuse them from doing the duties they are employed to do. That would be very bad business practice and very poor managerial practice. We are interested in identifying the price for the sole purpose of assisting the staff member to come to terms with the price and find ways to pay it. We need to do this for one reason and one reason only: in order to get more of the right things done.

In order to get the job done with the most excitement, commitment and dedication from our staff, we need to identify what the price is, and ensure that it is paid or put aside, but in some way taken out of the picture. The manager is in a good position to help the staff member pay the price, because it is easier for somebody on the outside to make suggestions than somebody who is actively involved in the problem. You probably know that when you are emotionally involved in a problem, it is difficult to see things clearly, and it is much easier for somebody on the outside to find solutions.

The second reason is that the manager often knows more about the situation than the employee does. That is why he or she was appointed as a manager, and he or she might well have suggestions to offer the staff member to make the problem go away. The time you spend helping the staff member pay the price is time very well spent. It might take you ten minutes, and this could save hours or even days of work done half-heartedly, reluctantly or without enthusiasm.

We want to know what the price is, not so that we can allow people to shirk their work, but quite the contrary so we can find solutions so that they can do their work. The old-fashioned manager who was not well trained probably would have said at this point: 'Well, they must just do it anyway.' That is an irresponsible and nonsensical answer, because people will not simply 'do it anyway'. If they are forced to do something, they will do it half-heartedly, reluctantly and poorly. What we want from our staff is that they are enthusiastic, committed, dynamic and excited. The only way we can do this is if we help them overcome the prices that they have to pay. The price has to be paid because the work has to be done.

Let's look at two methods for solving price-related problems.

Effective and Efficient Solutions

How do you know in advance that the solution you have come up with is a good solution? The answer to that question is 'with great difficulty'! We only know for sure that something is the correct solution after the fact, when it is all over. But that's not good enough. We need to have some way of thinking about solutions that allows us to select the best solution in advance. One way of doing this is a technique based on two notions: effective and efficient.

Whatever solution you come up with will not be a good solution unless it is effective. An effective solution is a solution that gets the job done. If it doesn't get the job done it is ineffective. Efficient means that it uses the least amount of energy or resources. The resources could be money, they could be goods, and they could even be time.

Let's consider an example and you can see how this can be applied. You notice that the performance of one of your staff members has been getting a bit sloppy. His mind doesn't seem to be on his work any more. So you call him into your office and talk to him. You find out that the problem isn't about clarity, commitment or self-image; it's about price. The man is having terrible problems at home. His wife has left him with three children, and two of them are sickly. She has walked off with the bank account and the car, and he is really taking strain. To ignore his personal problems and do nothing about them is too great a price.

'I'm going absolutely nuts,' he says, 'and I feel like my head is bursting! I really need some time out.' He asks if he can work half-days for the next two weeks, so he can have some time to sort out his problems at home.

The problem, in a nutshell, is that the man needs time out to sort out his personal problems. Now we need to find a solution. Giving him time off would be effective. But is it efficient to give him two weeks of half-days? If he has to come into work every day, he won't really be able to concentrate on his work or his problems at home. It would be more efficient to give him a full week off. Then he could stay at home the whole day and sort out his most pressing problems so he can get a handle on things. Also, if you give him Monday to Friday off, then he'll have nine days' break, because he has a weekend at either end of his week off, and it only costs you five days in lost productivity. So you have yourself an effective and efficient solution. He can attend to the most urgent issues, think them through, and get them out of the way so he can focus on his work even if the problem hasn't been resolved.

You are pleased with yourself because you have solved the problem and the man is happy, and so you get on with your work. Three minutes later, someone else comes into your office and says, 'I'm completely wrecked, I really need time out, I'm under such pressure at home.'

Problem definition: the man is deeply stressed and needs time out.

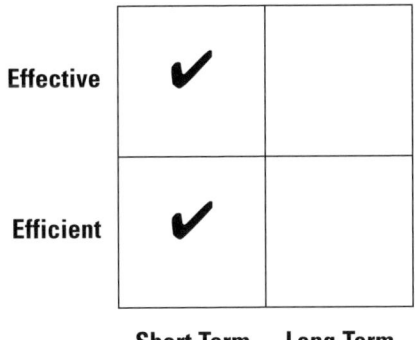

Short Term   Long Term

You look at this person and say: 'Who are you kidding? You just heard me give somebody else time off and now you want exactly the same thing!'

The staff member says to you: 'What do you know about my life? What do you know about what I'm going through?' Now you have yourself a problem! Everyone is going to ask you for time off to deal with their personal problems.

You see, when you came up with your effective and efficient solution, you only thought in terms of the short term. You didn't take the long-term implications into account. You set a precedent that is not sustainable in the long term. You have to set certain conditions to avoid this.

Instead, you might have said to the man: 'Look you are not ill, so I can't give you sick leave. But you are entitled to fifteen working days' leave a year. What I could do is give you five days' leave now and in December when we are always short-staffed you will only have a ten-day vacation.' Now you have an effective and efficient solution in the short term as well as the long term.

When another staff member comes over to you and says they need time out as well, you say: 'Certainly, if you need time out you should take it. How much time off do you need – two days, a week, ten days?'

The person looks at you and says: 'Ten days would be very good; that should do it.' And you say, 'Well, you take your ten days. But remember that over the December period, when we are always short-staffed, you will only have five days' vacation.'

By anticipating the long-term implications, you have designed a solution that is effective and efficient in the short term and the long term. As a manager you need to ensure that the job gets done. Your staff member was paying a price, and you helped him pay it, but in a way that the job still gets done.

Problem definition: the man is deeply stressed and needs time out.

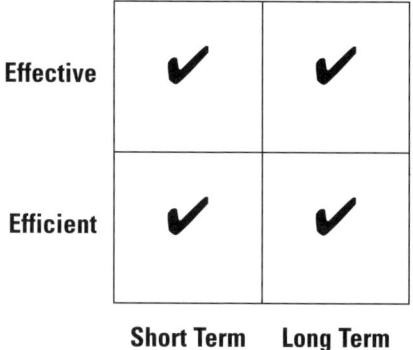

1 x 3 x 3 Problem-Solving Technique

Now I'm going to introduce another technique for finding solutions to price-related problems. It's a very versatile technique and you can use it in many contexts, not only for solving price problems.

For every problem you must identify three causes and for each of these causes three solutions. You can identify five causes or six causes, but you must always have at least three. For each cause you must have at least three solutions. The reason for this is that when people have a problem, they jump quickly to a solution, and the solution that they jump to is often wrong. This method makes you think more carefully and logically about problems, and helps you to find the best solutions. Then, using the effective and efficient method, you can pick the solution most likely to succeed.

1 Problem	3 Causes	3 Solutions

Here's an example. One of your sales staff is always behind with her paperwork. When she's face to face with customers she is excellent; she's in her element. But her paperwork is always a bit shoddy. Using the arch, you are sure that she knows clearly what she has to do, so you don't have a clarity problem. She seems to enjoy her work and is proud of being part of the company, so you don't have a commitment problem. There doesn't seem to be any self-image problem attached to doing paperwork. So you conclude that it is a price problem, and you need to find a solution to make the problem go away. We use the $1 \times 3 \times 3$ method for solving the price problem by finding the best solution.

You decide that the three possible causes of the problem are: one, she is not good with figures and is reluctant to do something she's not good at; two, she earns commissions for selling, not for doing paperwork, so she prefers to concentrate on selling; and, three, she finds paperwork boring, which makes her restless, so she is easily distracted and gets little done.

If the cause is that she is not good at figures and doesn't like doing what she isn't good at, then one solution would be to give her training to improve her skills. Secondly, she could swap roles with another sales person, so she does prospecting for him if he does her paperwork. Thirdly, she could hire an assistant for half a day per week to do it for her.

If she perceives the price of doing her paperwork as being the loss of sales she could be generating during that time, you could help her overcome the price by offering a counselling solution: counsel her on how paperwork is part of selling in the same way that driving to the sale is. In the time it takes her to drive there she could be making another sale. But she has to take the time to drive there, and similarly she has to take the time to do the paperwork to conclude the sales process. As a second solution, you could suggest she takes a company laptop with her to sales calls so she can do the paperwork while she is waiting to see the client. As a third solution, you could suggest that she do all her paperwork on Saturday when she can't see customers.

If the price is doing something she finds boring, you could assist her to overcome it by making the task less boring and more of a challenge by doing it quickly; or she could cluster all her paperwork on one day so that she knows she only has boring work on one morning, not every day; or you could advise her to arrange to sell on behalf of another sales person one morning in exchange for having him do her paperwork.

All the solutions suggested above would help her solve the problem of always being behind with her paperwork.

The $1 \times 3 \times 3$ method is a good way of finding possible solutions to a problem, by looking at the root causes of the problem. Once you have found multiple solutions, you can choose between them using the 'effective and efficient' technique. This will help you make good decisions that are effective and efficient in both the short term and the long term.

Staff members have to pay a price, and that is often the reason why they don't perform. By helping them pay the price, you will get better performance out of them. You will have happier staff and you will be a happier manager.

5

Behaviour

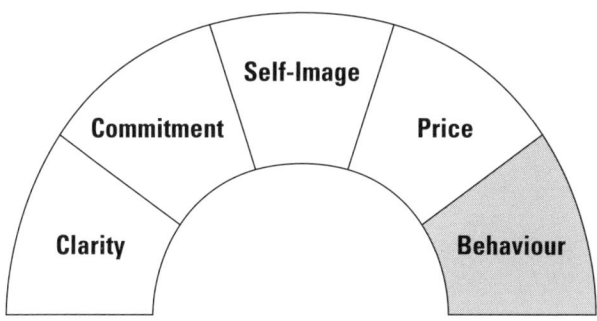

Sometimes the problem you have with a staff member is not a clarity problem: they know what you want them to do. Nor is it a commitment problem, for they are committed to their work, or a self-image problem: their self-image is right for the job. And it is not a price problem. Sometimes it is just a behaviour problem.

What do we mean by 'behaviour'? Behaviour is the way one acts or conducts oneself. It is not what you think, it is not what you want to do; it is what you actually *do*. When we think of behaviour, we must completely forget about the inner dimensions of the person. We are not interested in things like commitment or self-image; these we have dealt with. We are simply interested in what you do. Behaviour is the surface stuff that can be changed on the surface.

A behaviour problem can be as simple as a lack of knowledge or skills. You need someone to do a bank reconciliation, for example, but she doesn't know how to use the accounting package on your computer. This is something that can be solved by training.

If you went to Japan and were introduced to the MD of a large company, and you extended your hand and said you were pleased to meet him, you would be considered very, very rude. You have always prided yourself on your good manners and courteous behaviour, and now your Japanese host tells you that your behaviour is awful and rude. What did you do wrong?

In Japan, you are supposed to bow in greeting. The more important the person, the lower the bow. To stand up straight and put out your hand is to behave as a superior to the Japanese MD. You behaved inappropriately because you didn't know about this Japanese custom.

A behaviour problem could also be a lack of self-discipline, a lack of attention to detail or a lack of focus. It could be not knowing how to manage time properly, failing to listen to instructions, not getting around to carrying them out, and so on. In these cases, you might know what to do and how to do it, but you've just developed bad habits and so you just don't do it.

Bad habits can be changed. Behaviour can be taught and learned. If you have bad time-management skills, you can change that by keeping a diary, working out how long it takes to get to places, and leaving in time so you aren't late. If you are a bad listener, you can change that by taking notes when you are given instructions.

The point is that people can behave in a way that is not the same as the way they think or feel. It is possible for somebody to behave courteously, even if they don't feel like behaving that way. The person who keeps a diary and forces themselves to be on time might still have little natural concept of time, but nevertheless they behave appropriately. Behaviour is only what is manifest, what one does. Inappropriate behaviour can be changed.

IDENTIFYING A BEHAVIOUR PROBLEM

All too often, managers jump to the conclusion that a problem is a behaviour problem without first examining the four other possibilities – clarity, commitment, self-image and price.

If you have not made your instruction clear to a person, they cannot behave appropriately. If you tell a staff member to keep their work area clean and you haven't made clear what that means, then they cannot do it appropriately. If your instructions are not clear and the behaviour you get is wrong, you don't have a behaviour problem; you have a clarity problem.

If you have been very clear in your instructions and the person knows exactly what to do, but just doesn't care about it, you don't have a behaviour problem. You have a commitment problem.

It is easy to confuse a commitment problem with a behaviour problem. In order to get this clear we need to do a test. When somebody is not performing, you have to ask yourself whether the problem is a lack of willingness or a lack of ability. Lack of willingness is a commitment problem, and lack of ability is a behaviour problem; these are the same things using different words.

Imagine a mother who always tells her child that she is unable to help him with his homework because she has left her glasses at work. Let's look at this case in terms of the willing and able test. If she were simply tired when she came back from work, and did not wish to be bothered by her child, we would have somebody with a commitment problem. In other words, she is perfectly able to help him, but at the end of a working day, exhausted from a long shift, she is just not willing enough to do so. But there's another possibility. Perhaps she is unable to read. She is not unwilling to help the child; she would love to help him. The fact is that she quite simply does not know how to read. She has an ability problem; she doesn't know the behaviours that are required.

The reason it is so important to distinguish between commitment and behaviour is because very often we get annoyed with staff members and presume that they are not willing to do the tasks we have assigned them. We assume they are lazy, uncooperative or uncommitted, when in reality they might lack the ability to do the tasks because they haven't been properly trained.

If you are going to try to get people to change, to perform better, you need to understand the nature of the problem. If it is a commitment problem, giving them training won't help; you need to encourage them and press the appropriate hot buttons. If it is a behaviour problem, encouragement won't help; feedback and training will.

The amateur manager does not distinguish between commitment and behaviour, and often condemns people wrongly. The professional manager, understanding the difference, will be able to get to the heart of the problem, and thereby make the appropriate corrections.

A behaviour problem is also very different from a self-image problem, although the outcome might look the same. If you give someone a task that is above or below their self-image, they won't do it effectively. If, for example, a staff member has to study further to get ahead in their job, but they never did well at school and have never succeeded at studying before, their low self-image will tell them that they won't succeed and they will expect to fail. Simply to tell them that they must finish their course when their self-image says they cannot do it is usually a waste of time. Their refusal to study is not a behaviour problem, it is a self-image problem. To correct this you would have to raise their self-image by encouraging and assisting them so they feel that they can do it, that they can succeed.

If the person is clear about what they have to do, and they are committed to doing it, and there is no self-image problem, but still they don't perform, it could be a price problem.

A price problem occurs when there is a reason why the person cannot do what you request because doing it would be very difficult for them. If one of your staff members refuses to stay late to prepare for a promotion, this could be a price issue, not a behaviour issue. Their child's day care centre might close before they would get there, and the idea of their child waiting outside crying, feeling abandoned by their parent, is too high a price to pay. So they don't stay late.

You see, when someone doesn't do what you ask, there may be many reasons for this other than a behaviour problem.

Once we have eliminated all the other possibilities for under-performance or non-performance, we get back to where we started this chapter – with behaviour.

You can think of what behaviour is by considering things that you would want to change about your staff's behaviour. What would you like them to start doing, stop doing, do more of and do less of? These are all aspects of behaviour.

For example, Jay is one of the people in your department. What you would like him to start doing is taking more initiative. There are so many things that he is capable of doing, but he always waits to be told to do them. He should start doing these things without having to be told.

What you would like him to stop doing is coming late; he seems to be late more often than he is on time for work. When he is late he places a greater burden on the other staff who have to cover for him. It also affects the morale of the group when a person comes late. There might be problems of transport, but others from his area seem to overcome these; he should too.

What do you want him to do more of? You want him to be friendlier to customers, smile more, greet them more, chat to them more.

What you want him to do less of is chatting to colleagues when there is work to be done. It is important to communicate with colleagues, because that helps to create good feeling in the store. But Jay seems to spend an inordinate amount of time chatting to colleagues, even when there is serious work to be done.

Behaviour assessment

Behaviour / Name	Start	Stop	Do more of	Do less of
Jay	Taking initiative	Coming late	Being friendly to customers	Socialising when there's work to be done

Every part of the arch works on both you and your employees. If something is not going as you would like it to, you need to look at yourself and your staff in terms of each aspect of the arch.

You have to be clear about what you want from your staff, and you have to ensure that they are clear about what you expect from them. You have to be committed, and you have to help them develop their commitment. Your self-image has to be appropriate or you can't manage, and theirs has to be appropriate to the task, otherwise they can't do it. You have to be prepared to pay whatever price it takes to accomplish what needs to be accomplished, and so do they. And it is no different with behaviour.

There are ways in which you behave that are appropriate and useful, and there are ways that are not. In exactly the same way, there are ways in which your staff behave which are appropriate and useful, and other ways in which they behave that are not. So it works on both sides right throughout the arch.

Look at your own behaviour. If you think about it, you'll probably find that you are a long way, or at least some way, from being that perfect manager that you want to be. That doesn't mean you are not getting closer all the time, but you're not there yet. The gap needs to be bridged by, among other things, changing your behaviour. You need to think about what you need to start doing, stop doing, do more of and do less of.

But let's now look at how to change your staff members' behaviour, by means of feedback.

FEEDBACK

One of the most important ways of changing behaviour – in fact, one of the most important aspects of management – is giving feedback. Human beings learn how to deal with the world because of the way that the world responds to them. We act, and then we get a reaction. And based on that reaction we understand whether our actions are acceptable or unacceptable, appreciated or not appreciated, and that allows us to make a decision whether to carry on behaving like that or not. In the world of work it is exactly the same. The way we know what to do, and what not to do, is based on the feedback that we get from our colleagues, our managers and our environment. It is vital to give feedback to staff in order for them to perform well.

Most students of psychology have at some time or another done an experiment with rats, based on the process of stimulus and response. When the rat performs a certain act, it gets a reaction – a positive reaction like food, or a negative one like the withholding of food – and this changes its behaviour. The rat will learn to do what is being rewarded and not to do what is being punished. The closer the response is to the action, the faster the rat learns. In this respect, human beings are not very different from lab rats.

We are very much like yachts on the open seas. The yacht is probably off course most of the time, but it reaches its destination by zigzagging back and forth, going off-course and doubling back, constantly correcting.

Human beings need feedback from others in order to understand how they are performing, and what they are supposed to be doing.

The reason why some people perform so poorly is that nobody has bothered to tell them so. I suspect that well over half of all people who are underperforming don't even know that they are. If you find out at the annual development review that your manager doesn't think very highly of you, it is a little too late. We can change people's behaviour by giving them feedback as close as we possibly can to the time of the event.

Ken Blanchard, the author of *The One Minute Manager*, said: 'Feedback is the breakfast of champions!' Feedback makes champions out of people by letting them know what they should, and should not, be doing.

Sports people pay money to have coaches tell them what they are doing right and what they are doing wrong. Using their knowledge and experience, these coaches tell the sports person how to improve their behaviour – whether it is their serve, their pass, or whatever.

But people often dislike getting feedback, perhaps because it is badly given, or because it makes them feel humiliated and attacked. Managers, too, often dislike giving feedback, because they are too busy, too shy or unconfident, or because they don't want to hurt the other person. A manager who does not give feedback, for whatever reason, is not doing his or her staff members any favours. If a staff member is making a mistake, they will never learn, and will compound the mistake they are making. The manager is depriving them of growth.

What is the best way to give feedback? You must describe the staff member's behaviour fully and accurately, and you must make sure that you have all your facts. It is important that they know what was wrong – or right – about their behaviour. It is also important to give feedback as soon as possible so that the issue is still a concern to the person. Giving them feedback long after the event doesn't help much.

When you give a person feedback you need to be sure that you are building them up, not tearing them down. When you give negative feedback, you should do so in private, although positive feedback can be given in public most of the time. You must remain sensitive to how the person receiving it is reacting. You want them to do better after the feedback, not worse! You want their work to improve, not decline because they are angry or humiliated because of the way you conveyed your message.

An important principle for giving feedback is the 'next time' principle. In a book on leadership called *The Power Principle*, Blaine Lee writes about a school for delinquent children, which was run like a low-grade prison. The children, who were in for violent behaviour or drug abuse, were first placed in the lock-up, and then gradually earned rights and privileges as they proved themselves to be responsible. Blaine Lee observed a counsellor dealing with a child who had got into trouble when he and a few friends had broken out of the lock-up and tried to concoct an alcoholic beverage out of food and other stuff that they'd stolen from the kitchen.

Most of the conversation focused on what the boy would do the next time his friends encouraged him to do something wrong. The counsellor kept talking about 'next time'. Blaine Lee asked him about this later, and the counsellor explained that there was nothing he or the boy could do about the past. By talking about the past, he would only humiliate the boy even more. The only thing he could do was counsel the boy and give him skills to handle the next time his friends tried to entice him to commit a crime. The counsellor's task was to help him deal with the next time, not to humiliate him about the last time.

The 'next time' principle is the key to giving feedback that is intelligent, useful, and that will be appreciated and valued by staff members. There is hardly any point in rehashing the past. Once a person knows that what they did was substandard or wrong, the only issue is what they are going to do next time.

The Feedback Format

In order to give accurate and constructive feedback, you need to remember four words: WHEN, THEN, BECAUSE, THEREFORE. This is the format for good feedback. It allows you to organise your thoughts. If you can remember these four words, you will be able to give excellent feedback.

- **When**
  - What happened; just the facts
- **Then**
  - How I feel about it
- **Because**
  - The consequences of the action
- **Therefore**
  - What I want you to do in the future

When someone has done something wrong, you need to let them know accurately what they have done, why it is wrong, and what to do next time. The feedback format ends with 'therefore'. This is the 'next time' principle; you are focusing on the next time.

Follow me through this example of how you would use the feedback format for a reprimand. Let's say you asked a staff member to meet you after work. You agreed that you'd meet them in a shopping centre, next to the escalator at 6:30. You were there at 6:30, you were still there at 7, and they didn't show up. When you speak to them the next day you can either not say anything because you don't want to cause a fuss, or you can confront them.

You could start yelling at them, telling them how terrible they are, but you are not going to get the desired result. If you used the feedback format, on the other hand, you would say: 'WHEN we agree to meet at 6:30 at the bottom of the escalator in the mall and I wait until 7 and you still don't show up, THEN I get mad as hell BECAUSE I've wasted half an hour, had plenty of things to do and missed my transport back. THEREFORE, in the future if we make arrangements and you can't keep them please phone me on my cell and this is my number.' *When, then, because, therefore.*

One of the dangers of losing your temper and yelling at the person is that they could easily say: 'Oh, but we didn't agree to meet this Wednesday night; it's next Wednesday night.' If you used the feedback format you wouldn't feel as silly as if you had lost your temper and started yelling. That is one of the added benefits of using the feedback format.

Now, it's important to understand that we don't only give feedback when people are doing things wrong. You don't only want to stop people doing things wrong, you also want to get them to continue doing things right. This is also a way of changing behaviour. You tell them about their good performance so it becomes their standard performance. And you use the same feedback format when you want to reinforce good performance.

Follow me through this example. The manager asks somebody in the accounts department to put together a document describing certain aspects of the budget. The accountant gives her the document the next day, and she takes it to a meeting. When she comes back, she passes the accountant in the corridor and says: 'You know that report you gave me? Damn well done.' The accountant smiles and says, 'Thanks very much, I spent three-and-a-half hours working on it.' And the manager says, 'Yes, and it shows.'

Now, if you didn't know about the feedback format, you'd probably think she has done a great job – after all, she has just complimented the person. But let's go behind the scenes. What did the accountant spend three-and-a-half hours doing? He spent three hours designing a really attractive cover and getting the graphics exactly right. What did the manager enjoy about the report? The fact that there was an index that told her exactly where to find the various documents, the fact that all the supporting information and documents were at the back of the pack, and that on the very first page after the index was an executive summary of the central thrust of what the report was all about. That allowed everyone at the meeting to understand quickly what the report was about and find the relevant information very easily.

What is the accountant going to do next time? Next time he is going to spend three hours again designing the cover, but he might well change the way he arranges the content, which is the only thing that the manager appreciated. The manager has actually given vague and sloppy feedback, and because of this, the accountant will probably get the wrong message.

Let's see what the manager would say if she used the feedback format. She'd say to the accountant: 'WHEN you give me a report like the one you gave me this time, THEN I am incredibly impressed BECAUSE it had an index in the front, and an executive summary afterwards. All the information was clearly spelt out and the supporting documents were at the end, not spread throughout the report. This made it easy for everyone to understand the material. THEREFORE, in the future, whenever you give me reports, please follow exactly the same format, it was superb.'

The manager has used the feedback format – *when, then, because, therefore*. The accountant knows exactly what the manager enjoyed, what she wants, and what do next time. Feedback not only changes negative behaviour, but can also reinforce positive behaviour. This is also behavioural change.

It is important that you get used to using this format. When you first use it, it will be a little stilted, but after a while, the more you use it, it will start to flow naturally. Instead of saying, '*When* you do this, *then* I feel this, *because* of that, and *therefore* I want you to do this,' it will flow more easily. You'll find yourself describing what happened, how you feel about it, what the consequences are, and how you want the person to behave in the future. It will flow naturally and easily, like a conversation.

Feedback and Ego States

As is clear from what I've said so far, psychology plays an important part in giving and receiving feedback. Let's look at this in terms of the ego states we discussed in Chapter 3.

Very often when we have to reprimand someone, or give them feedback on substandard performance, we really don't know what to do. The amateur manager tends to go into child mode or parent mode, and both are inappropriate ego states for giving feedback.

The manager who goes into a child ego state will say: 'Look, I really don't mind, but you must understand that my GM is on my back all the time, and he doesn't like you showing up late all the time and not doing your job. Me, I don't particularly care. But he – he's the one – he's always on my back, so I have to tell you this.' The person receiving this type of feedback will look at the person giving it, and one word will come to mind – *wimp*.

Alternatively, managers will go into the parent ego state. They yell at the person, telling them how terrible they are. This is the mode of the old-fashioned manager. By addressing the staff member in this way, you push them into child mode. And if you humiliate a child, they become resentful and spiteful, and they don't do what you want them to do. You won't get an adult who hears what you say and takes your advice. You are paying an adult's wage and getting a child, which is never useful.

To get decent performance, you must deal with people adult to adult. The only way to give feedback is in an adult ego state, when you feel strong, unemotional, rational and objective. This will allow the other person to be in an adult state as well, so they can understand that you are giving them useful information. You don't want them to feel that their ego has been attacked.

Using the feedback format allows you to give quality feedback in an adult ego state, while maintaining the other person's adult ego state as well. It gives you some structure to help you deal with people.

What do you do when the staff member's ego state is inappropriate? If they go into child mode, you have to be very careful to relate to them *as if* they are in adult mode. Most often this will flip them into adult. You could say that you can still remember when you used to make this mistake and how pleased you are that it is behind you. That way, you are talking adult to adult about an issue that adults have to deal with along the way; not talking like a parent reprimanding a child for doing something wrong.

If the staff member goes into parent ego state, your only hope is to remain firmly in adult. Then they will drop back into adult mode too. If they say: 'Who do you think you are, telling me what to do?' you run the risk of going into parent mode yourself and saying: 'Don't you forget who I am! I am your manager and I will not have you talking to me in that tone of voice!' If you were in adult mode, you might reply: 'This is not a fight; we are just talking about getting work done correctly.' Or: 'Oh, knock it off, there is a job to be done, so let's think it through.' In both cases the focus is not on the person or the power play, but on the task. Feedback must be heavy on the behaviour and on the future, and light on the person.

Behaviour is the last thing you look at, once you are certain that a problem does not stem from clarity, commitment, self-image or price. Behaviour is the surface stuff; it is what people do. It can be learned and unlearned. By means of feedback, presented in a constructive way, you can correct your staff's behaviour, and ensure that they do the right things.

Conclusion

Managers are faced with people problems of some sort or another every day. That is why we have managers – to solve these problems. The manager who has no problems is fast asleep or completely out of touch with reality. Professional managers soon realise that the bulk of their work is solving problems, and to do that well they need to be equipped with a tool to analyse problems and find solutions. When managers have no tools, they usually try to guess what is wrong and condemn their staff members for being 'useless'.

The professional manager, like the professional doctor, must use tools, methods, ideas and knowledge to diagnose problems. The arch is a tool for managers to analyse managerial problems intelligently and effectively. It enables them to look at the situation, analyse what part of the arch is causing the problem, and find the appropriate solution.

Whenever you have a problem with a staff member – because they are not working as well as you would like them to, or because their job has changed and now they need to learn new skills or work in a new way – you need to refer to the arch to find out how to solve this problem. You have to analyse the problem, using the five elements on the arch.

On the left-hand side of the arch is clarity. You first need to ask yourself: Am I perfectly clear about what I expect from this staff member? You need to be clear about what you expect from them – so clear that you could describe it to another person in the amount of time it takes you to go from ground floor to first floor in a lift. That clear, that distinct. If it isn't that clear and distinct, then you need to rethink it and work out exactly what you want from them.

Once you are perfectly clear about what you want, then you can move to the next stage. You need to ask yourself whether the staff member is underperforming because they are not clear what you want from them. In other words, you are clear, but they're not. If somebody is not clear about what they have to do, they can't possibly do it. If that is the case, then you use the techniques that we discussed in Chapter 1 for making yourself clear to other people.

We looked at the CRIS model, which is a checklist for effective communication. You must check for clarity of communication, to ensure that the person has understood you. Then you need a reporting structure, a way of knowing if everything is on track, that is appropriate to the person's level of development. Then you need to involve the person to get their buy-in and their ideas, and finally set clear standards for the work you expect.

If clarity was the only problem, then once the person is clear, the problem will be solved and you will be a happy manager.

However, it is possible that both you and the staff member are clear about what has to be done, but still they are not performing as you would wish them to. Then you move to the next part of the arch – commitment – and ask yourself the question: Is this staff member committed to doing this task or activity? If they are not committed they will do it half-heartedly and poorly.

If you have a commitment problem, you need to address it using the techniques that we discussed in Chapter 2. You need to identify the person's hot buttons – the five most important issues at this stage in their lives – and you need to connect their work to their hot buttons.

Now let's presume that the person is clear about what needs to be done. They are also committed: they like you, they like the company, and the activity is important to them. Then you need to ask yourself the next question: Do I have a self-image problem here? A self-image problem occurs when the person's self-image is inappropriate to the task that you are asking them to carry out. You will recall that no one wants to do anything that is above or below their self-image, and if they do it, they seldom do it well. If you give someone a task that is too menial or too overwhelming for them, they will probably not do it, and if they do, they will do it reluctantly and poorly.

A self-image problem could also arise if the person is in the wrong ego state. You want your staff to be in an adult ego state, because then they are responsible, proactive and diligent. To achieve this you must remain in an adult ego state yourself. If you act like a parent to your staff, you will force them into child mode, and then you will not get good work out of them.

It is also possible that the person is perfectly clear about what they have to do, is committed to doing it, and has no self-image problems, but is still not performing. You then need to ask yourself, is it a price issue? Do they believe that they have to pay too high a price in order to carry out the task? If the price is too high, quite clearly they won't do it. If this is the case, you have to assist them in paying or removing the price.

If you've come to the conclusion that the problem is not clarity, commitment, self-image or price, the person might simply have a behaviour problem. Their behaviour is not appropriate and gets in the way. Behaviour is what a person does, not what they think or feel; it is the surface stuff that can be changed on the surface. To address a behaviour problem, you need to give feedback that is appropriate and constructive, using the feedback format that we discussed in Chapter 5.

You must also understand that sometimes the problem with the staff member does not stem from one of these factors, but a combination of them. It might be a lack of clarity as well as a self-image problem. It might be a commitment problem as well as a price issue. These problems are more difficult to solve, but the same principles and solutions apply. While the amateur manager is left guessing, the professional manager will use the arch to solve the problem and get the best out of his or her staff.

The important thing to remember is that you will not be a successful manager if your staff are unhappy and demotivated. The old-fashioned manager did not care about such things, thinking that staff must just do the job anyway. In this book I have shown you practical ways of working constructively with your staff and winning them over, and I have shown you how this will help you get the right things done. If you follow these principles and apply them in the workplace, you will be a more successful, effective and professional manager.